PREJUDICE
IN AMERICA

PREJUDICE IN AMERICA

Causes and Cures

by Michael Kronenwetter

Franklin Watts
New York/Chicago/London/Toronto/Sydney

Library of Congress Cataloging-in-Publication Data

Kronenwetter, Michael.
Prejudice in America: causes and cures/by Michael Kronenwetter.
p.   cm.
Includes bibliographical references and index.
Summary: Examines prejudice in our society and in
ourselves, looks at the damage it does, and explores
ways to overcome prejudice.
ISBN 0-531-11163-6
1. Prejudices—United States—Juvenile literature. 2. United States—
Race relations—Juvenile literature. 3. United States—Ethnic
relations—Juvenile literature 4. Minorities—United States—Juvenile
literature. [1. Prejudices.] I. Title.
E184.A1K838 1993
303.3'85'0973—dc20   93–1598 CIP AC

CONTENTS

Dear Reader

This book was written to help us think about prejudice. To recognize it in ourselves, in other people, and in society at large. To realize how it distorts the way we feel, and think, and act. To understand the damage that it does, not just to individuals, but to society at large. And, finally, to do everything we can to overcome it, in our hearts and in our lives.

Prejudice is not an easy thing to think about—and not only because it is a complicated and sensitive subject. It is difficult to think about because prejudice itself plays tricks with our minds. It distorts the way we see other people and the world we live in.

As hard as it is to think about, prejudice is even harder to talk about—and to write about. Anything you say is likely to be misunderstood and misinterpreted. We are all very touchy about prejudice: not only about the prejudices others feel toward us, but about any accusation that we might be prejudiced ourselves. And yet, it is vital to understand that we are all prejudiced to some degree.

In writing this book, I have been particularly worried that, by discussing prejudices and stereotypes, this book might reinforce them in some readers' minds. Even worse, it may plant them there. If so, that would be a tragedy.

Nothing in this book should lead anyone to believe that any racial, religious, or ethnic group is in any way inferior to any other group. If anything in this book seems to point that way, the author has not made himself clear.

But, no matter what the risks, they have to be taken. Prejudice is far too important—and dangerous—to ignore. It is something we must all force ourselves to think about, and to talk about, and to write about. And to overcome.

— Michael Kronenwetter

Chapter One
A KILLING ON SOUTH FIGUEROA STREET

Los Angeles, California—March 16, 1991

No one will ever know what Latasha Harlins was thinking about when she walked into the Empire Liquor Market that day. It could have been anything that any other fifteen-year-old girl might think about. A boy. A school assignment. Family troubles. Her plans for that evening.

Very soon, none of those things would matter anymore. Latasha Harlins would be dead. Her death would become a major event in the history of Los Angeles—the violent symbol of the fears and hatreds that divided two of the city's minority communities.

The events leading to Latasha's death were captured by a videocamera mounted above the door of the little store. The camera had been put there to discourage thieves. Theft of all kinds was a constant problem in this high-crime neighborhood of south-central Los Angeles.

Despite its name, the Empire Liquor Market on South Figueroa Street was as much a neighborhood grocery as a liquor store. There were at least two other customers present when Latasha walked in. Both were children, a brother and sister who were there on an errand for their parents. Like Latasha, they were black.

Attending the cash register behind the counter

was a middle-aged woman named Soon Ja Du. Born in Korea, she had been in the United States for about as long as Latasha had been alive, and she was an American now. She was more than an employee. Her family had owned the Empire Liquor Market for two years, and she had an owner's interest in what went on there. That was one reason she kept a close eye on the black teenager who had just entered.

Storekeepers in this neighborhood were in the habit of watching their customers—and particularly their young black customers—with intense suspicion. Soon Ja Du was no exception. Light-fingered "customers" were costing the little store, and her family, a lot of money. Many, if not most, of the offenders seemed to be teenagers from the neighborhood.

As the older woman watched, Latasha picked up a bottle of orange juice and slipped it into the backpack she was carrying. It was just as the shopkeeper had suspected. The girl was stealing from her. Sometimes it seemed that they were *all* stealing from her.

There had always been tension between the neighborhood's Korean-American storeowners and the African-Americans who made up the bulk of their customers. It was not easy for any small storeowner in this poor section of Los Angeles. Shoplifting, which was at least nonviolent, was the least of their problems. In the short time the Du family had owned this store, for instance, it had been held up three times, and burglarized forty times more. That made forty-three robberies in just two years!

In addition, there had been constant harassment by gangs of black teenagers, many of them no older than Latasha. But, as bad as things were for Soon's family, they were even worse for many others. Several Korean-American groceries in Los Angeles had been firebombed, and nineteen Korean-American grocers had been murdered in their stores during the past decade. It was no wonder that storekeepers of all backgrounds, and Koreans most of all, viewed their customers with wariness and anxiety.

The fear and distrust felt by the Korean-American storeowners was matched by the hostility of many of their black customers. As many neighborhood residents saw it, the Koreans charged too much, taking advantage of the fact that most people couldn't afford to travel to distant neighborhoods to shop.

Most stores in these poor neighborhoods charged too much, of course. But it was harder for blacks to accept when the Koreans did it. It was bad enough that African-Americans had to live in a country both owned and controlled by white people, they felt. Why should they have to put up with being dissed and ripped off by newly arrived Asians, too? And right in their own neighborhoods at that.

The Koreans argued that they needed to charge high prices in order to cover the cost of the constant thefts and damage. Things were so bad, they pointed out, that Koreans were often the only people willing to open food stores in the neighborhood.

Neighborhood residents admitted that robbery and vandalism were serious problems for the Koreans. But they felt that the Koreans shouldn't blame black people for that. Crooks were crooks, whatever their color. Besides, any store in a poor, drug-plagued neighborhood like this one was likely to get robbed. Didn't the Koreans know that black people got robbed and murdered, too? Black people got murdered more than anybody.

It wasn't just the high prices that irked many neighborhood residents, either. The Koreans took the money they made out of the black neighborhoods. They profited from the neighborhood, and then gave nothing back. Not even jobs. Koreans hired Koreans, the neighborhood people grumbled, not blacks.

What's more, the way the Koreans behaved toward their customers added personal insult to economic injury. The Koreans' manner was cold and neutral, when it wasn't openly rude. Black customers often felt treated with brisk hostility, even while the Koreans were taking their money. If you come to do business in somebody else's neighborhood, people insisted, the least you could do is be friendly.

The Korean-Americans believed that the African-Americans misunderstood them. If Korean-owned stores were usually staffed by Koreans, it was because these were family businesses. The owners couldn't afford to hire outside workers, whether black or any other color. They had to rely on their own family members just to keep the business going.

Storeowners claimed that they didn't mean to be rude. Koreans were brought up to be more formal, and less outgoing, than most Americans. Particularly most African-Americans. Neighborhood residents were too ready to mistake a Korean's businesslike attitude for hostility. They were wrong to take such differences in personal style personally.

All these angers, fears, and misunderstandings would play their parts in what was about to happen in the little store on South Figueroa Street.

Shortly after sticking the orange juice in her backpack, Latasha Harlins approached the cash register. She was carrying two or three dollar bills in her hand. It's not clear what she intended to do with them. She might have intended to pay for the orange juice (which cost $1.79), or she might have intended to ask for candy or cigarettes from behind the counter. Whatever she intended to do, she never got to do it. As soon as she arrived at the counter, she was angrily challenged by Soon Ja Du.

The videotape has no sound, but the two child witnesses reported that the Korean woman accused the black girl of stealing the orange juice in her backpack. When the girl protested, the woman reached out and grabbed hold of her sweater. Latasha struggled to pull free, but Soon held on and wouldn't let go.

What's the matter with this crazy woman? the girl must have wondered. *Can't she see I can pay? I've got the money right here in my hand!*

If the storekeeper called the police, Latasha might be in serious trouble. After all, who would the police believe? A respectable storeowner or a black teenager accused of shoplifting? Seized with fear and anger, Latasha struck out, hitting the middle-aged woman in the face with her hand. But the enraged storekeeper held on, and in the brief struggle that followed, Latasha smashed her fist into the woman's face again and again.

Finally, reeling with pain, Soon Ja Du released her hold, staggering backward to the floor. Half-stunned by the blows to her head, she grabbed a stool and flung it at the girl. Wracked by rage and terror, she reached under the counter for the .38-caliber handgun that the family kept there to defend against a fourth holdup. The gun was entrapped in a holster, however, and she had to struggle to pull it free.

Latasha, meanwhile, had bent down to pick up the orange juice that had fallen out of her backpack. It certainly wasn't worth all this. To show that she had no intention of taking it, she put it on the counter, but the older woman merely slapped it away. Abandoning all hope of making peace, Latasha turned and headed for the door.

But it was too late to escape. It was too late for everything. Soon Ja Du had finally managed to wrest the gun from its holster, and now she raised it up and pointed it toward the departing girl.

It went off.

The bullet smashed into the back of Latasha's head, and the girl dropped to the floor.

The storekeeper would later testify that she had never intended to fire the gun. She did not even remember the explosion of the gun going off. Evidence presented at the resulting trial would show that the firing mechanism of the gun had been worked on to make it easy to shoot—so easy that it might have gone off with no pressure at all on the trigger.

But, whatever the storekeeper's intention, the result was the same. Latasha Harlins was dead.[1]

Shockwaves

News of the killing sent shockwaves through the city's African-American and Korean-American communities. From the start, members of each group tended to make very different assumptions about the killing.

Most African-Americans saw Latasha Harlins as the innocent victim of a cold-blooded murder. They pointed out that she had been leaving the store when she was shot, and that she had willingly left the orange juice behind. Soon Ja Du, they believed, must have been blinded by racial hatred to kill a fifteen-year-old over such a petty thing as a bottle of orange juice.

Many Korean-Americans, on the other hand, assumed that Latasha Harlins was a thief who had attacked the storeowner who had tried to capture her. No one seriously argued that the girl had deserved to die for the theft of a bottle of orange juice, but the older woman had been under intense pressure. What's more, she had been under violent attack. Although few

Korean-Americans would defend Soon Ja Du's actions, one Korean-American declared, many understood them.[2]

Controversy over the case sparked several demonstrations and protests, and inflamed the hostility that already existed between Los Angeles' African- and Korean-American communities. A few months later, an African-American man was shot by a Korean storekeeper in another Los Angeles grocery, leading to a black boycott of Korean-owned stores. The Empire Liquor Market had already closed down soon after the killing.

The Verdict in the Courts

That October, a racially mixed jury found Soon Ja Du guilty of voluntary manslaughter: that is, of killing Latasha Harlins in the heat of passion. In addition, they found her guilty of using a firearm in the commission of a felony. Both crimes together carried a maximum possible penalty of fifteen years.

A probation officer who examined the defendant for the court recommended a heavy sentence. She reported that Soon Ja Du had showed no real regret for what she had done. On the other hand, both a psychiatrist and members of the Du family insisted that the woman felt real remorse for the death of Latasha Harlins.

In the end, Judge Joyce Karlin, who was white, gave the convicted killer a relatively light sentence: five years' probation, four hundred hours of community service, and a fine. She believed that the woman was, in fact, sorry for what she had done. The fact that the probation officer failed to recognize this, the judge declared, was "more likely a result of language and cultural differences than a genuine lack of remorse."[3]

Judge Karlin emphasized that Soon Ja Du was in

no way justified in killing the young girl. But the woman had been acting under "great provocation, co-ercion, and distress." The judge hoped that the Afri-can- and Korean-American communities would remember Latasha's death "as a catalyst to force [them] to confront an intolerable situation," and use it to help them find some way to heal the gulf between them.[4]

The Verdict in the Neighborhood

But the tragic death of Latasha Harlins didn't heal the gulf between the African- and Korean-American communities. Instead, it made that gulf into a chasm. Many black residents were outraged by what they saw as a slap on the wrist for a cold-blooded killer. To them, it seemed that the courts had put a terribly low price on the life of a young black girl.

"This is another assault on the quality of life and dignity of African-Americans," proclaimed a Los Angeles city councilman.[5] "We'll take this to the streets," an angry black resident declared.[6]

Some outraged citizens launched a drive to re-move Judge Karlin from the bench, to punish her for her leniency toward Soon Ja Du. The anti-Karlin activ-ists claimed that they were not acting out of hostility toward Korean-Americans. Their quarrel was with the American justice system, which, they maintained, has always been unfair to black people.

"I believe there are enough registered voters out there—black, white, green, or purple—who are upset and angry enough to put [Judge Karlin] out of office," declared Latasha's aunt.[7] Her litany of colors, however, did not include any shade that might apply to Koreans.

There is no real doubt that the anger in the black community was fueled, at least partly, by racial hostil-ity. Anti-Korean feeling was obvious from the boycotts

of Korean-owned grocery stores. Some Karlin supporters muttered that the protests were being fueled more
by greed than by outrage. Charles Matthews, who
headed a committee to defend the judge, charged that
some of the protest's leaders (not Latasha's family),
were using the anti-Karlin drive primarily "to collect
money from poor people." The leaders denied it.[8]

Inevitably, many Korean-Americans were angered
by the black community's response to the killing and
its aftermath. The death of Latasha Harlins was tragic,
they agreed, but so were the deaths of the murdered
Korean shopkeepers. "We haven't had a demonstration every time a Korean shop owner gets killed," one
offended Korean-American pointed out.[9]

Those Los Angelinos who refused to take sides
could only look on the dispute in sadness. "As I see
it," one member of the Los Angeles Human Rights
Commission commented, "there were three victims in
this whole situation." One, of course, was Latasha
Harlins, who had been shot to death. Another was
Soon Ja Du, who had been so terrorized, for so long,
that she was driven to kill. And the third was "the good
will between African-Americans and Koreans."[10]

Another Verdict

The truth of these words was proven a year later. In
April 1992, four white police officers were acquitted of
charges of beating up a black man named Rodney
King. Many Los Angeles residents, as well as other
people around the country, were shocked at the verdict. The fact of the beating was undeniable. Like the
killing of Latasha Harlins, it had been caught on videotape, which had been shown over and over again on
television. Within hours, much of Los Angeles erupted
into what became one of the worst riots in American
history.

Angry young African-Americans took to the streets of south-central Los Angeles to vent their frustration over what they saw as yet another abuse of justice. Once again, many of these rioters believed, the white power structure had shown its disrespect for their rights. The rioters, spurred by outrage at the verdict, were quickly joined by looters taking advantage of the chaos to steal and thrill-seekers eager to join the mayhem for its own sake.

Fires were started, and buildings were trashed and looted in several neighborhoods. Rocks and bottles were thrown at cars. White bystanders were attacked. For hours, the police stood by and left the streets of black neighborhoods to the rioters.

By the nightfall following the announcement of the verdict, many shops and other buildings in South Central were in flames, with new buildings being torched all the time. Mindless of the news cameras trained on them, scores of blacks, whites, and Hispanics rushed back and forth through shattered shop windows, staggering under the weight of stolen furniture and television sets.

Although no Korean had played any part in the Rodney King beating, Korean-American shops were specially targeted by many black rioters. Altogether, some eight hundred Korean-owned stores were trashed, looted, and even burned to the ground.[11] When asked why Korean-owned shops were being singled out, residents brought up all the old accusations against the Korean shopowners. The Koreans charged too much. They wouldn't hire blacks. They took money out of the black neighborhoods. But, most angrily of all, the residents brought up the killing of Latasha Harlins.

*   *   *

A single, powerful disease claimed the life of Latasha Harlins, led to the beating of Rodney King, and inflamed the Los Angeles riots of May 1992.

The name of that disease is prejudice.

Prejudice has plagued American society from the arrival of Columbus, if not before. The earliest European settlers on this continent despised the "redmen" they found when they arrived. They called them "savages," and treated them more like dangerous animals than like fellow human beings. Eventually, the Europeans' American descendants would import black slaves from Africa, despising them too for the color of their skins, and also for the place they came from.

In both cases, the whites assumed that because the Africans and Indians belonged to different "races," they were inferior. And that inferiority, they assumed, made it "all right" to treat them more cruelly than they would ever treat people of their own color and background.

It is particularly ironic that prejudice infects America. After all, the United States is a nation of immigrants, founded on the declaration that "all men are created equal." And yet, American history shows wave after wave of prejudice striking every new group of immigrants that arrives in this country. Then, as each new group becomes established here, it becomes equally prejudiced against those who arrive next.

Although the disease of prejudice has always existed here, it has been more virulent at some times than at others. Until the mid-nineteenth century, it was powerful enough to allow slavery to exist throughout the South. Until the 1950s, it was still strong enough to allow the legally enforced segregation (separation) of the races in much of the country. In the 1960s and the 1970s, on the other hand, a national commitment was forged to attack the disease. Although it was never completely wiped out, many of its worst symptoms were suppressed. Legal segregation came to an end, and laws were passed to force equal treatment of people of all backgrounds. It became socially unacceptable in most places to express hostility toward anyone because of his or her skin color or ethnic background.

Unfortunately, many of these advances seem to have been reversed in recent years. Social scientists tell us that the national commitment to overcome prejudice has weakened. Forms of bigotry that were once widely condemned as shameful have become socially acceptable again.

All of this means that it is now more important than ever to protect ourselves against this terrible disease. To do that, we must understand what causes it and how it infects us. That is the purpose of this book.

Chapter Two
AN INTRODUCTION
TO PREJUDICE

Ervin Staub, the author of a recent book on group violence, defines prejudice as "a strong negative evaluation of a group of people because of their membership in that group."[1] Not because of anything they do, or even any belief that they uphold, but simply because they are a part of some group.

This kind of prejudice is like some terrible disease that attacks not only individuals, but society as a whole. If we think of American society as a body, prejudice is like an infection that is raging through the bloodstream, attacking every organ and every cell. It is a disease that blurs the vision, destroys the judgment, and weakens the muscles and sinews that hold us together. At its worst, it is deadly—deadly enough to end the life of a young girl, and turn a middle-aged shopkeeper into a killer.

The Difference Between a Prejudgment and Prejudice

One popular dictionary defines the noun "prejudice" as "a preconceived idea, a judgment or opinion formed before the facts are known."[2] Another defines it as "a premature or hasty judgment."[3] As a verb, all sources agree, "prejudice" is almost always negative, meaning "to injure, or harm."[4] Prejudice, then, is a negative (or hostile) prejudgment.

There's nothing wrong with making prejudgments—even negative ones. We make prejudgments
all the time, and some of them are bound to be unfa-
vorable. An old warning against prejudgments warns
that "you can't judge a book by its cover," but we
frequently have to do just that.

Suppose you're at an airport newsstand and your
plane is about to take off. How can you choose a book
for the flight except by looking at the covers of the
books on the rack? When you see covers that don't
appeal to you, you'll reject those books and look for
another one. When you see a cover that interests you,
you'll probably buy the book.

Your judgment is really a prejudgment. You do
not have enough evidence to know which books are
good and which are bad. The covers could be misleading. A good book can have an unappealing cover,
and vice versa. Your judgment would certainly be better if you had time to look through each book before
making your decision, or even to sample a chapter or
two. But if you did that, the plane would leave without
you. As a practical matter, you have to judge the books
by their covers.

But the mere fact that you prejudge the books
doesn't mean that you are prejudiced against them.
According to Professor Gordon W. Allport, a Harvard
expert on the psychology of prejudice, a prejudgment
only becomes a prejudice when it is "not reversible
when exposed to new knowledge."[5] In other words, a
true prejudice is more stubborn than a simple prejudgment.

It is sometimes hard to be sure whether we are
prejudiced about something or not. One way to tell is
by whether we have fairly weighed all the available
evidence in forming our opinion. If we have honestly
examined all the facts we have, and if we are willing

to consider new evidence as it appears, we are not prejudiced. (We might still be wrong, but we are not prejudiced.) If, on the other hand, we ignore evidence that fails to support our opinion, then the chances are that we are prejudiced.

It is important to understand the distinction between an ordinary prejudgment and a prejudice. We have to make all sorts of prejudgments in our lives. We do not have to cling to our prejudices.

Acting on Prejudgments

Another important question to ask is how ready you are to take drastic action on the basis of little evidence. In general, prejudice makes us more willing to take strong action against someone, on the basis of less evidence, than we would otherwise.

Suppose you're walking down the street, and you see a man with a gun in his hand running out of a bank and firing back into the building. No matter what your race or his, you're probably going to make some very quick prejudgments about him. First of all, you'll probably assume that he is robbing the bank or engaging in some other serious criminal activity. What's more, you're going to assume that he is dangerous, and act accordingly. (You might slip into the nearest doorway or dive under the nearest parked car.)

You actually have very little solid evidence for these assumptions. You could be wrong about the man. He might be a policeman instead of a robber, firing back at criminals inside the bank. He might even be an actor, playing out a scene for the benefit of cameras you haven't noticed. But, even though you might be misjudging him, you are not reacting out of prejudice. In fact, you have more than enough evidence to justify taking action to protect yourself.

You do not, however, have enough evidence to

justify harming the man, since you don't really know who he is shooting at, why he is doing it, or even if the bullets are real. Even if you had a gun of your own, you would not have a good enough reason to draw it and fire on him. And, assuming that you are not prejudiced against him for some other reason, you probably would not do so.

So far, in fact, there has been no question of prejudice. Whether your judgment of the man is right or wrong, you are making it on the basis of his personal behavior, not on the basis of any group to which he belongs. But suppose you and the man have different skin colors. If you are prejudiced against people of his color, you might feel more certain of your negative assumptions about him—more ready to take out your own gun and shoot.

First Impressions

We've all had the experience of taking an instant liking, or dislike, to someone. Such quick judgments are almost always premature. We rarely learn enough about a person, the first time we meet, to form a fair opinion of the person. And yet, we *do* form an opinion, almost immediately. In fact, it's almost impossible *not* to make some kind of judgment about a person the moment we meet, however tentative the judgment might be.

Most often, first impressions are based on something very superficial: the way people look, the clothes they happen to be wearing, their size, their accent. In reality, these things say very little, if anything, about the real character and worth of an individual. And yet we often base judgments of new acquaintances on them.

The reason we tend to judge people by such factors is obvious. All we know of most people we meet is what we see on their surface. Even after we know someone for a while, we might find out little about the person beyond what we can see and hear. As a psychology textbook explains: "the other person's surface is sometimes the only clear thing about him."[6]

Most first impressions are prejudgments, not true prejudices. This is because they will usually quickly give way to experience. In some cases, this experience will confirm our original judgment. The person turns out to be just as likable or unlikable as we first thought. Sometimes, however, we find that our first impressions were way off the mark. Someone we immediately trusted betrays us. Someone we instantly disliked turns out to be a friend. It's even common to hear married couples admit they couldn't stand each other when they first met.

But sometimes our negative first impressions remain with us, even when nothing happens to support them. Sometimes, in fact, first impressions are so strong that they cannot be changed by further experience. Even when someone we distrusted on sight turns out to be honest and reliable, we still find ourselves hostile and suspicious toward them. In such cases, we are no longer laboring under a first impression. We are feeling an active prejudice.

How Prejudice Works

There are different kinds and levels of prejudice, and different prejudices affect us in different ways.

A prejudice might be experienced as a virulent hatred: *Jews are scum who should be wiped off the face of the earth.* It might produce an amused contempt, such as: *The natives are like innocent children.* Or it might only lead to a vague sense of discomfort: *White people are all right, I guess, but I can't really relate to them.*

Most of us don't recognize our prejudices for what they are. Some of the most prejudiced of us would deny that we are prejudiced at all. Instead, we *assume* that we have good reasons for our hostile attitudes about other people, even if we can't explain those reasons logically. In many cases, however, we have no real reasons for our feelings at all. Just excuses.

As much as anything else, a prejudice can be a feeling: an attitude. We are uncomfortable around people of another religious or ethnic group. We don't know why, but they make us uneasy. So we make up stories that we tell ourselves to justify our uneasiness. *Fundamentalists aren't as smart as we are. Hungarians are dishonest. Blacks are dirty. The Japanese are obsessed with sex.* Anything to explain—and justify—our feelings of discomfort to ourselves.

Some of us are frightened of people of another race. We have no specific reason to be. No member of that race has ever done any harm to us. But still we feel the fear. So, once again, we make up stories to tell ourselves about them, such as: *You can't reason with those people. A lot of them are on drugs. They'd just as soon rob you as look at you.*

When our prejudices become so strong that they blind us to reality, we become bigots. Bigots are willing to deny, or simply ignore, virtually any fact that threatens to contradict their prejudices. A prejudice may be little more than an unjustified opinion, but bigotry carries the weight of emotion behind it. While prejudice leads to unfriendliness, bigotry leads to intolerance and hatred—the desire to see others come to harm.

The Desire to Be Different

No matter how our prejudices reveal themselves, they all have one thing in common: the desire to be different from some group or groups, to separate ourselves from those we are prejudiced against.

We sometimes treat that separation as a kind of

physical, or geographic, barrier: I *don't want those people near me. I don't want to live near them. Or to go to school with them. Or visit in their neighborhoods.*

Sometimes, we want a kind of social barrier: I *don't mind being around them, but I'm not going to be friends with them. Or date them. Or marry them.*

But, no matter how else we think of it, the distance is essentially psychological: I *am not like them. They are not like me.*

The Desire to Belong

As we have seen, prejudice makes us want to separate ourselves from some other group of people. It is as though we build a psychological fort around ourselves, to keep members of that other group out. But, since we feel uncomfortable inside that fort alone, we want to include others inside with us. This makes us assume that our prejudices are shared by a host of other people, with whom we identify ourselves. "I am not like them" becomes "*we* are not like them." Our psychological fort doesn't just keep the alien (foreign) groups out, it holds in those we identify with. This makes us feel safe.

Just as we see those we are prejudiced against as different from us in some essential way, we see those we identify with as like us in some essential way. We belong to one group. They belong to another.

Before long, we no longer see fully distinct human beings when we look at members of an alien group. Instead, we see primarily the thing that makes us define them as belonging to that group. At the same time, we no longer see members of our own group as distinct individuals either. With them and even with ourselves, we see mostly a single characteristic. *They are black, we are white. They are Catholic, we are Protestant. They are foreigners, we are Americans.*

Although we don't always think about it in these terms, we usually regard the objects of our prejudice as lacking something—something that *we* have. Something that is an essential part of what *we* are.

A homosexual isn't a whole man. Blacks don't have all the mental faculties that we whites do. Women can be very intelligent, but they don't have the mental toughness that we men have.

Varieties of Prejudice

Almost any characteristic can define a group. This means that virtually anything that distinguishes one person from another can be the spark that ignites prejudice against them.

Some men are prejudiced against women, for instance. Some women are prejudiced against men.

Ordinary-looking people are often prejudiced against those who are physically unattractive, and sometimes against exceptionally beautiful people as well.

Some wealthy people look down on anyone who is poor.

Some adults consider all teenagers irresponsible, immature, and ignorant.

Some healthy people feel repulsed by anyone with a physical defect or disability.

Some people consider anyone with epilepsy "weird."

Many city-dwellers feel contempt for "farmers," or those they define as "hillbillies" or "rednecks." Many rural Americans look on all city-dwellers with suspicion and fear.

These are just some of many common prejudices. The varieties of prejudice are virtually endless. Most often, the greatest victims of prejudice are the weakest and most vulnerable elements of American society— particularly racial, religious, and ethnic minorities.

Tribal Tensions

Ancient prejudices were often tribal. Many modern prejudices are essentially tribal too. Whenever we think of ourselves as members of a gang, or a nationality, or even of a particular race or religion, we are identifying ourselves as members of a modern tribe.

The simple act of dividing into groups, or tribes, establishes a gulf between us. It creates an "us" and a "them." We don't necessarily separate ourselves in this way out of hostility toward anyone else. Instead, we do it as a way of defining ourselves. "It's really [a search for] identity," explains Joe Giordano, of the Proud To Be Me program in Sarasota, Florida. "The real question is: 'Who am I?' "[7]

Identifying with a group helps us to understand who we are ourselves: I *am like these people*. This is especially important when we are young and desperately seeking to figure out where we fit into the world at large. This is one of the main reasons young people tend to form cliques at school, join street gangs, enroll in the Boy Scouts and Girl Scouts, or even go out for team sports.

Most psychologists agree that this desire to belong is both natural and useful. It is a good thing for us to recognize our fellowship with other human beings, to feel a part of some group larger than our families. But the search for tribal identity rarely stops there. We are not satisfied with defining ourselves by the groups to which we belong. We also define ourselves by the groups to which we don't belong: I *am not like those people*. And, for many of us, particularly for those who are young or insecure, it is reassuring to change that "I" into a "we": "*We*" *are not like* "*them*."

Identifying with certain other people doesn't necessarily mean liking them. We might very well dislike some members of our own group or tribe. Maybe even lots of them. (Members of ancient tribes didn't all like each other, either.) But we feel as though we have something particularly vital in common with them. We feel comfortable among them in ways we don't feel comfortable among other people. This sense of familiarity can lead us to accept them in ways we do not accept people who belong to other groups. It can also lead us to reject people who do not belong to our group.

In a sense, every group is exclusive. That is, it *excludes* people who do not belong to it. Every group is an in-group, to which some people belong and others don't. This implies that there are also out-groups, to which other people—those who are "not like us"—belong.

Discrimination

We might not feel particularly hostile toward members of other groups at first, but the mere fact that we exclude them tends to produce prejudice against them in the long run. Once we bar someone from our group, we need to justify our lack of hospitality, if only in our own minds. Even if we had nothing against them before, we now start to think of them as being inferior in some way. Undeserving. Unworthy. Even as bad. It is no longer just: *We are different from them*. It becomes: *We are better than they are*.

This leads us to react differently to people, according to whether they belong to our in-group or to an out-group. And it is only a short step from reacting differently to treating them differently.

Once we come to believe that people are inferior to us, we stop treating them as well as we treat those we think of as equals. When our group is larger or more powerful than theirs, we may even use our power to deny them the rights and privileges we demand for ourselves. This is what is called discrimination—the unfair treatment of one group of people by another.

One of the worst effects of prejudice is that it helps us to justify discriminating against others. *After all*, we tell ourselves, *We are better than they are, aren't we? We deserve more than they do, don't we?*

What Abraham Lincoln said about the United States over a century ago is still true today. "A house divided against itself cannot stand." Racial, religious, and ethnic prejudices are creating great cracks and fissures in the foundation of our national house. If the damage is not repaired, the house could come crashing down.

Fear

At bottom, most authorities agree, prejudice is rooted in fear. Fear of the stranger. Fear of the unknown. It is a hostile response to what we see as foreign, as different from us—and, therefore, as dangerous.

The fear of strangers was probably born in the depths of the great prehistoric forests. It was there that wandering hunters learned to stay alert for any sound or shadow that might betray the approach of some ferocious beast, or some even more ferocious human enemy. One of the main reasons our distant ancestors banded together into tribes in the first place was the desire for mutual protection—for safety from outside threats, from strangers.

Ever since prehistoric times, there has been a tendency for individuals not only to identify with members of their own tribe, but to be wary of outsiders.

Early tribal societies were relatively simple, and the differences between them were simple as well. Some ancient European tribes, for example, roamed about hunting for their food. Others stayed in one place, fishing and harvesting wild-growing plants. Modern anthropologists, who study ancient societies, believe that the more peaceful fishers and gatherers often had good reason to fear the hunters. In some cases, evidence suggests, hunting tribes committed virtual genocide against the fishers and gatherers, wiping whole tribes out of existence. Under the circumstances, it wasn't surprising that tribes became wary and suspicious of each other. Simply belonging to another tribe made you a potential enemy. Prejudices and group hatreds developed.

Once nations began to form, and borders were drawn, the fear of outsiders became a fear of foreigners. The descendants of hunters, who feared strangers coming to steal their kill, became citizens of nations who feared invading armies coming to conquer them. In some cases, of course, this fear was justified. But in other cases, it wasn't. Not all strangers were hostile, and not all foreigners were bent on conquest.

Those strangers who seemed dangerous were regarded with hatred and loathing, while those who seemed harmless were regarded with amusement or contempt. Both responses were signs of prejudice. Many people have similar reactions to foreigners today.

The more complex nations became, the more differences developed, not just between different societies, but between different groups within individual societies as well. And each of those differences became another possible spark for prejudice. By now we have developed all kinds of group differences, all kinds of "reasons" to be prejudiced against each other.

At bottom, however, every prejudice boils down to the same simple-minded proposition: *We are better than they are. Our tribe is better than their tribe.*

Chapter Three
RACIAL, RELIGIOUS, AND ETHNIC PREJUDICES

All forms of prejudice are wrong-headed and irrational. Every kind of prejudice infects us with an unjustified dislike of people we don't even know. But racial, religious, and ethnic prejudices are the worst of them all. They are particularly unfair, because membership in these groups is involuntary. Race and ethnic identity are determined by birth, while religion is a matter of faith.

Throughout history, these are the prejudices that have caused the most massive human suffering and the greatest injustices. They have contributed to a wide variety of human ills, from the cold-blooded cruelty of slavery to the viciousness of war. And, even today, they continue to threaten the quality of life of societies around the world—including here in the United States.

The Idea of Racial Superiority

From the beginning, skin color has been the single most pervasive cause of prejudice in American society. This country was born in conflict between the white European settlers and the Native Americans they called "redmen." Centuries later, while the struggle between the descendants of the Europeans and the Native Americans was still going on, the members of the Constitutional Convention were strongly divided over the question of enslaving black people. That issue would not be decided until the bloody War Between the States. Even after that, for a century more, racial segregation of the blacks remained a festering wound until it was cauterized in the violent struggle over civil rights in the 1950s and 1960s. And, in the years since then, life in virtually every large American city—and many small ones—has been blighted by what are often referred to as "racial tensions."

Skin color has long been identified with the idea of races: the idea that there are separate categories of human beings, whose different skin colors mark other, more important differences as well. Until fairly recently, even many scientists believed that people could be divided into distinct racial groups, whose members shared specific mental, emotional, and moral characteristics, along with the obvious physical ones.

If the races are so different, some people believe, then some must be better than others in various ways. One race must be more intelligent, one more ethical, and so on. In the nineteenth and early twentieth centuries, a group of scientists known as eugenicists set out to prove this theory. Because most of them were Europeans, they assumed that the "white" race was superior in most important respects. To prove it, they concentrated on what they saw as the differences between people of European and African descent.

They examined every difference they could find, or imagine, between these two groups. They measured the shapes and sizes of skulls, the widths of noses, and the textures of hairs. Some became convinced that they had established their theory, but their evidence is laughed at today. One nineteenth-century English entomologist (insect expert), for instance, argued that black people and white people must belong to different animal species because they attracted different kinds of body lice![1] Despite their best efforts, the eugenicists could come up with no evidence that can stand the test of modern scientific examination.

"Most social scientists regard scientific racism as dead,"[2] declares sociologist Robert Moore, of the University of Aberdeen. The anthropologist Leonard Lieberman, of Central Michigan University, agrees. "In anthropology, 'race' is more than halfway toward rejection and deposition in the museum of antique concepts."[3] According to most modern scientists, the apparent mental and moral differences some people believe exist between races can all be explained by social, educational, and economic factors that have nothing to do with race as such.

Understanding "Race"

What most nonscientists actually mean when they say "race" is skin color, combined with certain other physical characteristics commonly identified with similar-colored skins. "Black" people, for example, are said to have thick lips and broad noses. "Yellow" people are said to have slanted eyes. "Red" people are said to have high cheekbones.

Obviously, people do have differently-colored skins, and some physical traits are more often associated with certain skin colors than others. But none of these things are reliable ways of identifying one race from another. A great many "black" people have thin lips and noses, for example, while many orientals have rounded eyes.

Even color is not nearly as distinctive as people think. Although the races are commonly described as "white," "black," "yellow," "red," and "brown," skins actually come in many more shades than those. Some individuals of the so-called "white" race are actually darker-skinned than some individuals of other races. Even children of the same parents can have different shades of skin, so it would be absurd to claim that each skin color represents a significantly different race.

As Pierre L. van den Berghe has pointed out in his book *Race and Racism*, "It is not the presence of objective physical differences between groups that create races, but the social recognition of such differences as socially significant or relevant."[4] In other words, these differences are only important when— and if—we think they are.

Nonetheless, prejudice based on race—or color —has existed for a long, long time. Historically, people whose enemies have had different skin colors have used that fact against them. The myths of some ancient peoples claim that their enemies' skin color was a punishment brought on by a curse.

Some tribal cultures, including at least a few North American Indian tribes, considered themselves fundamentally different than—and superior to—the people of other tribes. In some tribal languages, in fact, the word for tribe members was the word for "human beings." Everyone else was called by another name, suggesting that they were some other kind of creature altogether.

When the Mongols overran China in the thirteenth century, they considered themselves racially superior to the native Chinese.[5] The Tutsi tribe in central Africa took its racial superiority over other tribes for granted long before any Europeans arrived in the region.[6]

But, even though race/color prejudice has existed in many times and places, the heavy emphasis some Americans and Europeans put on race today is very unusual. As far as we can tell, many ancient societies were totally free from racial bigotry. And, even where it did exist, it was rarely a major social problem. People had prejudices, but the way they felt about people of other colors had little effect on their actions. There was little, if any, actual discrimination.

This didn't really change until the colonial age, when the conquering Europeans found race prejudice a useful ally in ruling peoples of various skin colors all over the world. The idea that their race was superior helped them to justify their conquest, and the often cruel treatment that they inflicted on the native peoples. Prejudice was so closely tied to colonial attitudes that the term "native" itself came to have a belittling, even racist, ring to it. And yet, the core meaning of "native" is not racial at all. It merely means someone who was born in a particular place. We are all "natives" of somewhere.

Miscegenation

Color prejudice often shows itself in people's reactions to miscegenation: that is, to the idea of sexual relations between men and women of different races. Many people of all races oppose such relationships, particularly those leading to marriage and children.

In the United States, the strongest opponents of miscegnation tend to be white supremacist organizations like the White Aryan Resistance and the Ku Klux Klan. Believing that the white race is superior, they campaign against what they call "race-mixing." They complain that it "pollutes the blood" of both races, and call everyone of mixed races "mud people."

But white racists are not the only ones who oppose such relationships. Some members of minority races have similar beliefs. Many others resent their members who marry outside their race. They see miscegnation as a form of desertion. When Clarence Thomas became the second black person nominated to the Supreme Court of the United States, some black people argued against him on the grounds that he had a white wife. "His marrying a white woman is a sign of his rejection of the black community," declared Russell Adams, the chairman of the Afro-American studies department of Howard University.[7]

Renee Brokaw, a white woman who is married to a black man, told Newsweek magazine that she finds that a lot of otherwise very liberal people "still draw the line at couples. Integration for them means that they go to school together, but God forbid your son and daughter should date."[8]

This is a frequent reaction of families on both sides of interracial relationships. Both sides are worried, or even angry, about the union. Some feel that it is wrong to mix the races, while others claim that it is unfair to the children, who will face discrimination in later life.

The same argument is raised against any kind of mixed-race family, including those in which a couple of one race adopt children of another race. "There is bound to be prejudice from people of both races," say the opponents. "The children will grow up insecure and confused about their own identity."

The same point is often made by minority members who oppose allowing white families to adopt children of other races. In 1972, protests by The National Association of Black Social Workers resulted in a drastic reduction in the number of interracial adoptions.[9]

Children in interracial families do face prejudice, of course. Some also have problems dealing with their racial identities in a society that puts so much emphasis on race. But so do many minority children raised in one-race families. The best evidence we have suggests that the problems of being an interracial child are usually less serious than the critics of interracial families believe.

Caroline Wachira, the child of a marriage between a black man from Kenya and a white woman from England, is happy with her interracial status. "I realize that each person I meet is not a black or white statistic but a unique human being with hopes and fears as real as my own."[10]

Perhaps the best evidence on the question of interracial adoption comes from Rita Simon, a sociologist who conducted a twenty-year study of African American children adopted by people of another race. "[O]verwhelmingly," she reports, "these kids say the adoption experience was positive. They grow up whole people, mentally healthy and aware of their black identity."[11]

Racism

Some people use the terms "race prejudice" and "racism" to mean the same things. Others reserve "racism" for extreme racial prejudice: the kind that leads to hate crimes, and to the oppression of one race by another.

When critics charge that America is a fundamentally racist society, they don't just mean that many Americans are prejudiced. They mean that America's social institutions are set up in a way that favors the white race. According to these critics, the way our society is structured makes sure that white people keep control of most of the wealth and power. When they say "racism," then, what they really mean is racial oppression.

Some minority members use this definition to excuse the prejudices that they themselves feel toward other races. As members of a minority, they argue, they are the ones being oppressed. They are not the oppressors. Therefore, they cannot be racists.

In this special sense of the word "racist," only the most powerful race can be considered racist. Using this definition, some people insist that only white people can be racists in the United States. They are the only ones with the power to discriminate. "I don't see how I could be racist," a member of a black heavy-metal band told MTV. "I'm on the oppressed side of things."[12]

Some black political leaders who have been accused of prejudice against Jews also argue that they *can't* be racist because they are black. Somehow, they seem to imply, it's all right for them to be prejudiced. It's all right for them to hate another group. The fact that others are prejudiced against them justifies any prejudice they may feel toward anyone else.

Ultimately, this argument doesn't hold up very well. The same African-Americans who insist that they cannot be racists, argue that Jewish and Asian-Americans are racists against them. But Jews and Asians are also minorities in America. It is both sad and ironic that the three men whom columnist Jack Newfield of the *New York Post* has called "the three biggest anti-Semites in the country"—Congressperson Gus Savage, Minister Louis Farrakhan, and Professor Leonard Jeffries—are all black.[13]

The Latasha Harlins tragedy proves that race prejudice in America is not simply a white disease. So does the trashing of Korean stores in the Los Angeles riots. Many Asian-Americans are clearly prejudiced against African-Americans. Many African-Americans are also prejudiced against them. Many Americans of all other races are prejudiced against Native Americans, Latinos—and, for that matter, white people. In fact, the first person sentenced under a Wisconsin law providing harsher penalties for crimes motivated by racial bigotry was black. He had been convicted of encouraging several black teenagers to attack and beat up a fourteen-year-old white boy.[14]

Most hate crimes, however, are still committed by white people.[15] And, since they are the ones who have the most power in the United States, it is their prejudices that do the most harm. Even so, we must never forget that everyone is vulnerable to someone else's prejudice—someone else's hate.

Intolerance toward members of any race, people of any color, is clearly wrong. It is always wrong to judge other individuals, not by their own actions and character, but the color of their skin, whatever color that skin might be.

Ethnicity

Ethnicity refers to heritage. Everyone belongs to at least one ethnic group. Which group, or groups, you belong to usually depends on where you, or your ancestors, come from. An ethnic group can be defined in several different ways. By a common national or regional background. By common traditions and beliefs. By a common language. Or even by having similar skin colors.

An ethnic group can be large or small, and one group can include smaller groups. Italians, for example, make up a single ethnic group: and yet, that group includes the Sicilians, the Neapolitans, and several other groups, each of which has its own distinct traditions and practices. Native Americans make up an ethnic group, as does each of the many tribes and cultures within it. There are more than 1,500 ethnic groups on the continent of India, each separated by a distinctive language or dialect, although all of them can also claim to be Indians. With all the racial divisions in the world, with more than 180 countries, and over 6,000 languages, the number of ethnic groups is virtually uncountable.

In the United States, the term "ethnic group" is most often used to describe the so-called "hyphenated Americans." That is, the many groups—like the Irish-Americans, Mexican-Americans, Italian-Americans, and so on—who are still identified with the country from which their ancestors came to America.

Most Americans belong to several ethnic groups at once, although we usually identify more strongly with one than with the others. Some Americans, on the other hand, never think of themselves as members of an ethnic group, although just being an American makes us members of that national ethnic group. What's more, we're all either Native American Indians, immigrants, or the descendants of immigrants. Still, many of us do not add any mental hyphens when we think of our nationality; and except for those of us who are distinctively ethnic in appearance or accent, our ethnicity is not always recognizable by those around us.

The more we emphasize our own ethnicity, the more we are likely to be identified as ethnics by our fellow Americans. And many of us do just that. We glory in our cultural heritage, and take every opportunity to show it off. Many Irish-Americans celebrate St. Patrick's Day with parties and parades. Native Americans wear their hair in traditional styles. Scots-Americans attend Scottish festivals, where they wear traditional tartans, listen to bagpipes, and sing Scottish songs. German-Americans hold Oktoberfests, reveling in beer and bratwursts. And so on.

Other Americans, however, do their best to avoid identification with their ethnic roots, fearing prejudice, or even discrimination. There is some reason for this fear. A large number of Americans dislike, or disparage, anyone they consider *too* ethnic. They regard them as "foreign," as somehow not American enough. This attitude can be extremely illogical, particularly when some of the bigots are people whose families are more recent immigrants to this country than the "ethnics" they detest. But then, one of the main signs of prejudice is that it is unreasonable.

Religion

Religious prejudice is different from the other prejudices discussed in this chapter, in the sense that it is the only one directed against groups that people choose to join. You can't choose which race or other ethnic group to which you belong, but you can, if you wish, choose your religion.

On the other hand, many religious people would argue that religion is not really a matter of choice at all. It is a matter of faith. You can't honestly choose to deny your true beliefs. In any case, religious prejudice is just as unfair, and as destructive, as tribal prejudices of any other kind. It is also specifically un-American, since freedom of religion is a fundamental American right, as stated in the Constitution.

Of all the excuses for prejudice, religion is the most ironic. Virtually all of the world's major religions teach against prejudice. Christianity, Islam, Judaism, and Buddhism, among others, all preach love, tolerance, and the brotherhood of everyone. And yet, world history is full of examples of people who hated each other—and even slaughtered each other—over their religious beliefs.

This apparent contradiction can be partly explained by what Gordon Allport has described as the "perhaps unresolvable" conflicts between the beliefs of some religions.[16] The heart of those conflicts is the belief that one's own religion has possession of the absolute truth.

People who believe this are often convinced that they alone know God's will. They alone are right about the most fundamental questions of morality, and everyone else is wrong. For some, it is only a few short steps from this belief to a deep prejudice against everyone who believes anything else. After all, the reasoning goes, if everyone else is wrong about morality, everyone else must be immoral. And if they are immoral, they must be against God. And if they are against God, then it is only right to hate them.

Some people believe that they and others of their religion are specially favored by God. They feel that they have been selected by God to defend the truth against unbelievers. God, they feel, is on their side. It's just one more short step from believing that you have been specially selected to believing that everyone else has been rejected. And if God has rejected them, shouldn't you reject them too?

When people of one religion become dominant in any country, that country's laws and traditions tend to reflect the teachings of that religion. Inevitably, to some extent, the majority imposes its will on the minority who believe otherwise. In Italy, for example, divorce was outlawed for centuries because Italy is mainly a Roman Catholic country, and the Roman Catholic church opposes divorce. As a result, all Italians, whether Catholic or not, were forbidden to divorce. Even today, married women in some Middle Eastern countries have few legal rights because the dominant Islamic religion teaches that authority in marriage belongs to the man.

In those countries where one religion dominates, leaders of that religion tend to become spokespeople for the majority culture. Where their religion is supported by the government—as the Roman Catholic religion is in certain Latin-American countries—many of its leaders tend to support the government in turn. They preach obedience to state authority, and tell the people that political rebellion is a sin.

On the other hand, where a religion is persecuted by the government—as the Catholic religion was in Poland until recently—religious leaders tend to oppose the government and encourage the people to resist. In either case, political, cultural, and religious beliefs all seem to get jumbled up together. Disputes that have nothing to do with religion become inflamed by religious passion. And ethnic and religious prejudices tend to feed on each other.

Religion, itself, is not a form of prejudice. Nor does it inevitably lead to prejudice. For many people, religion leads in exactly the opposite direction. After all, it is a fundamental belief of many religions that all human beings are children of the same God, and that God loves everyone. This is one of the most powerful of all arguments *against* prejudice of any kind.

So, while religion feeds prejudice in some people, it destroys it in others. In fact, many of the most determined enemies of prejudice in human history—from Jesus Christ, who called on everyone to love their neighbors, to Gandhi, to the Rev. Martin Luther King, Jr.—have been religious leaders.

Religious prejudice exists in the United States, but fortunately, it is not as much of a problem here as it is in many other places. On the other hand, it does tend to affect and intensify other forms of prejudice. When we went to war in the Persian Gulf, for example, it was easier for some Christian Americans to feel hostile to the Iraqis because they were Muslims rather than Christians "like us."

Anti-Semitism

Anti-Semitism is prejudice against Jews. It shares elements of all the varieties of prejudice discussed above because there are many different definitions of what makes a Jew a Jew.

Judaism is a religion, and the people who practice it are Jews. Anti-Semitism, then, can be considered a religious prejudice. And yet, many Jews are not religious at all. What they share most is a cultural heritage, often passed down through many generations in either the Hebrew or Yiddish language. To that extent, Jews can be considered members of an ethnic group, and anti-Semitism can be defined as a form of ethnic prejudice.

Some anti-Semites consider Jews members of a distinct race, although there are black African Jews as well as light-skinned Jews, and Jews in other "races" as well. But, to the extent that the anti-Semites consider Jews a race, anti-Semitism can also be considered a form of racial prejudice.

The most extreme anti-Semites, like those in the so-called "Christian Identity" movement, define "Jew" in some extremely peculiar ways. One "Christian Identity" leader actually considers Jerry Falwell, the conservative Christian evangelist who founded the Moral Majority, to be a Jew because Falwell "believes in Israel."[17]

Many American anti-Semites claim to be Christians, and argue that their hatred of Jews comes from their belief in the Bible. The Jews denied Christ, they say, and crucified him, thus cursing themselves forever. This is the reason some anti-Semites refer to Jews as "Christ-killers."

In order to accept the supposed biblical basis for anti-Semitism, however, Christian bigots ignore the fact that the Bible was almost entirely written by Jews. They also ignore several key aspects of the biblical account. Most significantly, Christ was a Jew. So were Mary, Joseph, and the great majority of the followers Christ personally recruited to his cause. Although the Bible reports that some powerful Jews plotted against Christ, and that one of them betrayed him to the authorities who killed him, those authorities were not Jews but Romans. He was tried by Romans, under Roman law, sentenced to death by a Roman official, and executed by Roman soldiers. (Crucifixion was a Roman, not Jewish, method of execution.)

Many Christian anti-Semites never notice the contradictions between believing in Christianity and hating Jews. They simply don't think that much about it. Others go to absurd lengths to argue that those contradictions don't exist.[18]

The most extreme anti-Semites even deny that there is any historic link between Christianity and Judaism. Their arguments sometimes reach such dizzying heights of sheer silliness that they fall off the other side. According to the Christian Identity movement, for example, it is not modern Jews, but white Anglo-Saxon Americans who are the biological descendants of the Israelites of the Old Testament.[19]

Almost every major Christian leader has denied that Jews, as a group, bear any guilt for Christ's death. And yet, many people who call themselves Christians still cling to this twisted interpretation of the Bible, which has done more than anything else to spread anti-Semitism in the western world.

The Holocaust

Anti-Semitism fueled the most massive and murderous outburst of prejudice and hatred in the twentieth century: the so-called holocaust that took place in Nazi-occupied Europe in the 1940s. Adolf Hitler and the Nazis who controlled Germany at that time blamed the Jews for all the country's problems. Not long after Germany launched its effort to conquer Europe in 1939, Hitler ordered his officers to draw up a plan to kill all the Jews on the continent. It was to be, as Reich Marshal Hermann Goering put it, "the final solution of the Jewish question."[20]

The Nazis never publicly declared what they were doing, but they quickly began rounding up Jews, not only from Germany but from the countries they conquered as well. Anti-Semitism was so widespread at that time, that there was little protest as Jews all over Europe were jammed into the boxcars of trains and shipped to special camps designed to murder them.

After the war, most of the people who witnessed the arrests and transportations of the Jews denied that they knew what would happen to them. Most likely, they had no knowledge of the details. But they surely knew that their neighbors and friends were being unjustly arrested and taken away. And it was equally clear that none of them ever came back. Yet, fear and prejudice kept most of the non-Jews of Europe silent.

Some Jews were forced to work themselves to death as slave laborers. Others were used as guinea pigs for cruel medical experiments, in which they were frozen alive or operated on without anesthetic to test the limits of human pain. Most of the rest were simply herded into mass gas chambers, designed to look like ordinary showers, and put to death. Their naked bodies were sometimes thrown onto huge piles and then bulldozed into mass graves.

The Nazis failed in their attempt at genocide (the murder of an entire race or people), but they did manage to kill over half the Jews in Europe, along with

millions of other people they considered their enemies. No one knows the exact number of the Nazis'
victims. There is not even a reliable estimate. There
were—literally—just too many bodies to count. But
somewhere between five and six million Jewish men,
women, and children were killed without mercy in just
a few short years. Roughly half were slaughtered in
the death camps. Nearly another million and a half
were shot. Most of the rest perished when Jewish
neighborhoods, like the one in Warsaw, Poland, were
bombarded, set on fire, or otherwise demolished.[21] It
was the most extreme example in modern history of
the horrors that can result from prejudice.

Chapter Four
CAUSES OF PREJUDICE

Prejudice is a disease, and everyone is both a victim and a carrier of that disease. It is an infection that attacks us as individuals and attacks society as well. At times, the infection is relatively mild. At times, it is severe. Left untreated, it can be deadly.

Just as a physical illness can have many different causes, the mental and emotional sickness of prejudice has many causes as well. The most important of these is fear.

Fear of the Stranger
The fear that helps to produce prejudice today is not very different from the fear that hounded the ancient hunters thousands of years ago. Directly or indirectly, we usually see the people we are prejudiced against as a threat. And fear of the stranger, the other, the outgroup, is widespread in America today.

Anyone walking down certain city streets at night is likely to feel some fear. There is not necessarily anything bigoted about that fear. In a high-crime neighborhood, fear is a realistic reaction to a potentially threatening situation.

But not every neighborhood, even in a big city, is dangerous. In fact, most neighborhoods are not. If one is afraid simply because the neighborhood is unfamiliar, or simply because most people who live there belong to a different race, then the fear may be little more than prejudice.

Many white people are wary of any neighborhood with a lot of black or Hispanic residents, thinking *They are different from me. They are dangerous.* At the same time, they tend to feel safe in neighborhoods where most of the faces they see on the street are white. *They are like me, so here I'm safe.* But not every minority neighborhood is filled with crime, and the overwhelming majority of black and Hispanic people are no threat to anyone of any race. By the same token, not every white neighborhood is safe.

In some areas of the country, blacks and other minorities live in some physical fear of white people. In regions of the country where lynchings were common in the past, and where racial attacks still happen today, black people are often wary of white strangers they encounter on a street at night.

In the halls and playgrounds of many American schools today, whites, blacks, Hispanics, and Asians eye each other with suspicion and fear.

It is often hard to tell when such fears are realistic and when they are the reflections of a deep-seated prejudice.

Another kind of fear reveals itself in a common prejudice against physically or mentally handicapped people. When I see a homeless woman huddled in a doorway, or a man who has no arms or no legs, I might feel repelled as well as sympathetic. Beneath that sense of revulsion is fear. Not fear *of* the person. Fear *for* myself. *That could be me. That could happen to me.* We are often prejudiced against people who remind us of things about ourselves we would rather forget. In this case, it is our own vulnerability to disability that frightens us. But that fear makes us hostile to people whose only fault is to be victims of the very thing that frightens us.

The Dread of Change

Not all fear is physical. Some is social, or even economic. People often fear the effects that the arrival of new groups might have on their neighborhood or community. Many whites, for instance, resist the arrival of minorities in previously all-white neighborhoods out of fear that the newcomers will bring a lowering of property values and perhaps a general worsening of living conditions. *Will they bring crime and drugs into the neighborhood? Will they put out the garbage and cut the grass as we do? Or will they let their buildings disintegrate and leave old junk to rot away on their lawns?*

But it is not only whites who worry about other groups moving into their neighborhoods. Residents of minority neighborhoods often have similar feelings about the arrival of other minority groups. Or even members of the white majority. All newcomers are seen as the bearers of a different culture, different attitudes, unreliable standards, and strange habits. *Will they take over the neighborhood? Will my kids be safe on the streets?*

Even newcomers who are unlikely to lower conditions in the neighborhood might change them. For people with low incomes, newcomers who threaten to raise property values can be as frightening as those who might lower them. *Will I be ashamed of my house, compared to theirs? Of my old car? Will they make improvements that raise property taxes? Will I be able to afford to live here anymore?*

At the very least, things are bound to change. It will not be the old neighborhood anymore. Things that have been familiar and comfortable will be different now.

Many of the same fears and hostilities underlie the widespread prejudice against immigrants. In recent decades, this prejudice has been directed mostly against Latin-Americans, Asians, and Haitians, but at various times in the past it was directed against the Irish, the Italians, and other European ethnic groups too. *What will they do to the country? What kind of values will they bring?*

To some extent, these hostilities are territorial as well. *This place is ours. Those people have no right to it.*

It is natural for people to have some concerns about new arrivals in their neighborhood or community. After all, newcomers *do* mean change, and the change might not be always for the better. But prejudice makes us assume that the changes are bound to be for the worse, and inflates them out of all proportion to reality.

Economic Competition

Prejudice is likely to increase when jobs are scarce and there is fierce competition to get them. This is one of the main reasons that hostility toward immigrants rises in times of economic stress. Workers worry that the newcomers will take jobs away from those already here.

Other forms of competition also help encourage prejudice. Some college students, for example, resent the presence of so many Asian-Americans in graduate schools. There are only a certain number of places available in medical, law, and business schools, and in recent years students of Asian heritage have been getting a high proportion of them. Although the Asian students have been earning these positions with hard work and better grades, some whites and non-Asian minorities have convinced themselves that the Asians' presence is somehow unfair.

Surprisingly, economist Thomas Sowell states, prejudice is often most felt between groups that are most alike in certain ways. He points out that Irish and black Americans have had much in common. At different times in their histories, they have faced very similar economic problems and also similar prejudices against them. They even have similar cultures in many ways. "Yet despite these similarities—or perhaps because of them—blacks and the Irish have had the greatest hostility, violence, and bloodshed to exist between any two ethnic groups in American history."[1]

This seems less odd when you remember that groups that are very like each other are apt to be in direct competition. Hostility is often particularly strong among minority groups fighting for the same jobs. "Blacks think we want to take jobs away from them," a Chicano labor activist complained in 1991, "so they're fighting us tooth and nail. They are doing the same thing to us that whites did to them."[2]

The Need to Make Sense of the World

Fear—of strangers, of change, of competition—is rarely enough to cause prejudice all by itself. It is usually accompanied by ignorance and personal insecurity, as well.

The modern world is a complicated and confusing place, and American society is like a miniature version of the world as a whole. It is filled with people who look different, act differently, speak differently, and think in all kinds of mysterious ways. Most of us find the job of sorting out all these differences mind-boggling. We feel a need to simplify the world: to reduce it to simple formulas that make it easier to understand. Prejudice provides us with these formulas. They are called stereotypes.

It's scary to think that my neighborhood (much less the world) is made up of a whole range of individuals, most of whom I don't know and cannot hope to understand. But if I can convince myself that everyone of a certain color or background is alike—if I can believe that all black people are inferior, that all Jews are sneaky, that all Italians belong to the mob, and so on—I can feel more secure. I'm no longer adrift in a sea of mysterious strangers. I know who everybody is. I know where I stand with them. Or at least I think I do.

According to Richard W. Brislin of the Cultural Learning Institute in Honolulu, stereotypes like these "allow individuals to organize and structure their world in a way that makes sense to them."[3] What's more, they allow us to turn other racial or ethnic groups into scapegoats.

Clearly there are great evils and injustices in the world. How can these things be? The real answers to such questions are hard to find. They involve complicated social, economic, political, and spiritual forces that are probably impossible for any of us to understand fully. But not understanding can be frightening. So, instead of trying to make sense of these very real and complicated causes, many of us find it easier just to find a scapegoat. Someone to blame.

The American economy is having trouble? *It's a conspiracy of Jewish bankers.*

There is terrible poverty among Native Americans who live on reservations? *It's a white plot to wipe out the Indians.*

The American car industry is collapsing? *The Japanese are being unfair to us.*

Crime is exploding in the inner cities? *Blacks are animals who have no respect for life.*

I see a young Hispanic driving a brand new Mercedes, while all I can afford is a used Ford Festiva? *He must be a drug dealer or a pimp.*

Stereotypes and scapegoating don't just help us explain the problems of the world. They give us an excuse not to do anything about them. They relieve us of any sense of personal responsibility or guilt. Everything is someone else's fault. *If black people are poor, it's because they're too lazy to work harder. If Hispanics are poor, it's because they have too many children. If Indians are poor, it's because they drink too much.*

The fact that these explanations are false is not particularly important to the bigot. What is important is that they are *understandable*. They give her or him explanations for realities that would be too confusing and frightening to face without one.

Prejudice as a Substitute for Self-esteem

For some people, prejudice provides a handy substitute for self-esteem. There is a high correlation between prejudice and a poor self-image,[4] and bigotry often conceals a deep self-loathing.

"Racism stems from nothing more than self-hatred," David Cevette, an ex-member of the Aryan Nations white supremacy group, explained to reporter Doug Clark of the Spokane *Spokesman Review*. Cevette himself had a change of heart when he realized what his own self-hatred was doing to him. "I realized that I had no right to hate myself and then begin to hate other people," he said.[5]

Elie Wiesel, the Jewish survivor of Nazi death camps who won a Nobel Peace Prize in 1986, also notes the connection between bigotry and self-hatred. "Ultimately," he declares, "whoever hates, hates his brother. And whenever one hates his brother, one always hates himself."[6]

People like Cevette (before his change of heart) find it hard to take pride in themselves, so they take a pathetic kind of pride in their race or ethnic group instead. They cannot think about their own accomplishments, because they don't feel they have any. But they can take a kind of pride in the accomplishments of others. *See those successful people? See that business tycoon? See that great athlete? See that famous TV star? I belong to the same group as they do. I'm one of them.*

At the very least, bigots can take pride in the fact that they do not belong to some other group. *I may not be a success, but at least I'm white and not black. Or at least I'm black and not Asian. Or at least I'm a native-born American, and not just an immigrant.*

Some bigots cling to their prejudice because of the twisted sense of superiority it gives them. They see their contempt for minorities as proof of their own self-worth. *If they are bad, then I must be good.*

In reality, however, prejudice can never build true self-esteem. It can only undermine it. The bigot's argument is a phony one, and deep down he or she must know it. *If the only thing that gives me value is the fact that someone else is worth even less than I am, then I must not be worth very much myself.*

Chapter Five
STEREOTYPES

Picture a group of Native American Indians dancing.

What image comes into your mind?

If you're like most non–Native Americans, you probably see a group of men, dressed in deerskins and feathers, performing ceremonial movements to the beat of a drum. They might even have painted faces, and be carrying lances or bows and arrows.

This image is a stereotype.

The late columnist Walter Lippmann called stereotypes "pictures in our heads."[1] But stereotypes are not ordinary pictures. They are more like caricatures and cartoons than photographs. Instead of representing actual people or events, they represent certain beliefs, or assumptions, that we hold about whole groups.

The mental picture of the dancing Indians doesn't represent any specific Indians. It represents Indians in general. It isn't saying, *This is the way these particular Indians are dancing at this particular moment.* Instead, it's telling you, *This is the way Indians dance.*

But, like most stereotypes, this picture is misleading. Some Indians actually do dress up in traditional outfits and perform ritual dances. They do it for various reasons: as an exhibition for tourists, or as a ritual in a religious ceremony, or simply to keep an old tradition alive. But most Indians never dance like that at all. For the most part, they do the same dances, in pretty much the same ways, that other Americans do.

It would probably surprise many people to learn that "America's first great prima ballerina" was an Osage Indian. Her name is Maria Tallchief, and she was the leading ballerina in the United States for many years before becoming one of the founders of the prestigious Chicago City Ballet company. Maria's sister Marjorie was also a leading ballerina.[2]

Examples of Stereotypes

A typical stereotype assigns a specific quality, habit, or characteristic to everyone in a particular group. Whatever the characteristic is, the stereotype exaggerates it. Whenever artists draw caricatures of the comedian Bob Hope, they make Hope's ski-slope nose the main focus of the drawing. That is how people recognize that these lines and shapes are meant to represent Bob Hope. In the same way, a stereotype focuses your attention on one trait or characteristic which you see as defining a whole group of people. This characteristic can be either positive or negative.

Here are some examples of common positive stereotypes:

☞ Jews are intelligent.
☞ Americans are inventive.
☞ Protestants are hardworking.
☞ Japanese are industrious.
☞ Irish "have the gift of gab."
☞ Black people are good singers and dancers.
☞ Women are sensitive and intuitive.

But negative stereotypes are even more common than positive ones, and you are probably aware of many such stereotypes (unless you have led an extremely sheltered life).

Some stereotypes are two-sided; they are both positive and negative at once. It is a stereotype, for example, that Jews are exceptionally good at business. But, in the mind of an anti-Semite, this stereotype implies that Jews cheat those they do business with.

Some stereotypes seem neutral. That is, the behavior or traits they suggest don't seem to be either good or bad. But, in fact, neutral stereotypes often have a hidden, negative prejudice built into them.

Take the stereotype of the dancing Indians described above. On the surface, it might seem totally neutral. After all, there is nothing obviously good or bad about doing an ancient ceremonial dance. And yet even that apparently harmless stereotype contributes to a kind of belittling of the Indian people. It implies that Native Americans are simple, old-fashioned people incapable of adjusting to the modern world. Worse, it feeds what Indian activist Rudy Martins calls "the most painful myth" of all about American Indians: the myth "that we don't exist anymore."[3] To the extent that we associate them only with ancient dances, we imply that they are relics of the past.

Even apparently positive stereotypes can have damaging effects in the real world. Asian-Americans, for example, are often stereotyped as the one racial minority that does better in most ways than the white majority. But, as Patrick Anderson, the editor of *Asian Week*, explained to *USA Weekend*, this stereotype that presents Asian-Americans as "the ideal minority" actually "plagues the Asian community." It ignores the real problems of adjustment and discrimination many Asians face in America today. It implies "that Asians are doing better so they don't need help; the result is they're often left out of affirmative action programs."[4]

The Ugly American

White Americans tend to think of stereotypes as things that apply only to someone else. It is often a shock for Americans who travel abroad to learn that many foreigners stereotype Americans as much as Americans stereotype them. It is even more of a shock to find that those stereotypes often apply to Americans of all races. For many foreigners, Americans are Americans, whatever their color or ethnic background.

The traditional stereotype of people from the United States is summed up in the phrase "the ugly American." It pictures us as wealthy and spoiled people who think our money can buy us anything, and who always expect to have everything our own way. Traveling abroad, we flash our money around and think we can bribe or bully the people who live there into doing whatever we want them to do. As individuals, we tend to be boorish and pushy, with no appreciation of other cultures.

Lately, this stereotype has been changing. With America's increasing economic troubles in the past few years, the old view of the wealthy American is being replaced by a new view of Americans as fat, complacent, and falling behind the times. This new stereotype is particularly common in Japan, where a government official recently told the Japanese parliament that America's economic problems are caused by the ignorance and laziness of American workers. American employers, he maintained, can't even give their workers written instructions because so many Americans can't read.[5] Many foreigners believe such stereotypes, just as many of us believe equally unfair stereotypes about them.

Clinging to Our Stereotypes

We often attribute our own worst faults to the people we stereotype. If I am greedy, I will naturally assume that other people are greedy too. If I lie, I will assume that others are probably lying to me.

In the nineteenth century, most white Americans thought of the Indians as sly and untrustworthy. The term "Indian-giver" came into use to describe someone who broke a bargain. To white Americans, it implied that Indians were liars who couldn't be relied on to keep an agreement. In reality, however, it was the United States government, and not the Indians, who repeatedly broke the treaties made with Indian tribes.

This is typical of negative stereotypes. We use them to blame others for behaving in the same ways we behave ourselves. (Or, sometimes, in ways we would *like* to behave if we thought we could get away with it.) It's as though we want to see our own faults in others to avoid recognizing them in ourselves. If we identify a particular fault as belonging to *those other people*, then we do not identify it in ourselves. We *are different from them*.

In order to keep up this self-deception, we try hard to see people in our own group in the best possible light, and people from other groups in a much worse light. This trick of mental vision is necessary, because prejudice defines us by our differences. In reality, of course, no group is made up of interchangeable members, all of whom are either good or bad.

As long as we have little or no personal experience with individuals from other groups, it is relatively easy to maintain our stereotypes of them. But wide personal experience with many different individuals quickly begins to undermine our stereotypes. We are forced to see that all members of a group are not alike. Some of them will be very intelligent, some very unintelligent. Some will be kind, some will be cruel. Some will be strong, some weak. Some will be generous, some selfish. Some will be honest, some dishonest. Just like the members of any other group—including our own. In fact, if we allow ourselves to view people from other groups honestly, many of them are very much like many of us.

How do we maintain our stereotypes? One way is to judge people by standards assigned to the group to which they belong. We do this by interpreting behavior according to whether it is *ours* or *theirs*.

In war, for example, *our* side carries out a lightning raid, but *their* side launches a sneak attack. We move back in a strategic retreat, but *they* run away to save their skins.

The very same characteristic that we consider a virtue in ourselves, we consider a fault in them. We mask this hypocrisy by using different terms to describe what is essentially the same characteristic:

☞ We are intelligent. They are sly.
☞ We are ambitious. They are greedy.
☞ We are firm. They are stubborn.
☞ We are sensitive. They are soft.
☞ We are self-sacrificing. They are weak.
☞ We are diplomatic. They are dishonest.
☞ We are frank. They are rude.
☞ We are easygoing. They are lazy.
☞ We are outgoing. They are pushy.

It isn't that there is no difference between being intelligent and being sly, or between being ambitious and being greedy. These words can describe very different qualities. But when our thinking is distorted by prejudice, we don't see the real quality, whatever it may be. We see only the version of it that fits the picture in our heads—the stereotype that we are struggling to hold onto.

Exceptions Don't Prove the Rule

Once a stereotype is locked into our mind, we comb our experience for any evidence that helps us maintain it. We notice things that tend to support our prejudice, and disregard anything that tends to contradict it. We make assumptions that force the world to fit our prejudices.

Many anti-Semites are convinced that Jews are dishonest in business dealings. So, if an anti-Semitic customer is short-changed by the clerk in a dress store, she will assume that the clerk must have been Jewish. *This proves it*, the anti-Semite tells herself. *Jews are cheats, just as I always suspected.*

Facts and events that do not fit in with our prejudices are either ignored, denied, or explained away. The anti-Semite described above may have purchased things from a hundred Jewish people, each of whom behaved with scrupulous honesty. But she will not even remember those occasions. Only the event that supports her prejudice—or that seems to support it—will make an impression on her.

White supremacists will tell you that black people are mentally inferior to other races. If you point out that there are many highly intelligent black people, they will belittle them. *Maybe a few*, they will admit, *but they are just genetic oddities.*

What about Ralph Bunche? you might say. Bunche was an African-American who helped write the United Nations charter in 1945. Bunche later won the Nobel Prize for Peace, in an age when African-Ameri-

cans could not even drink from the same water foun-
tain as white people in many American states. Well,
the bigot will say, *he was an exception.*

What about Dr. Desmond Tutu of South Africa,
and the Rev. Martin Luther King, Jr., two other black
men who won Nobel Prizes? *Two more exceptions, I guess.*

What about Dr. Charles Richard Drew, who helped
invent the blood bank system that saves countless
lives every day? What about George E. Carruthers, who
invented the ultraviolet camera/spectrograph? What
about Thurgood Marshall, the great lawyer who became the first black justice of the Supreme Court?
What about Toni Morrison, Alice Walker, and Gwendo-
lyn Brooks, three black women who each won the Pulit-
zer Prize for Literature? *More exceptions.*

No matter how many prominent black scholars,
scientists, and artists you name, the confirmed bigot
will dismiss them all. *They are just exceptions,* the bigot
will insist, *and such exceptions prove the rule.* But, as any
scientist will tell you, exceptions don't prove a rule.
They *disprove* it.

What is true of black Americans is true of other
racial, ethnic, and religious groups as well. Members
of every race have made great accomplishments in
a variety of fields, achievements that contradict the
stereotypes.

It is true, of course, that such great achievements
are unusual. Most Native Americans will not become
great ballet dancers. Most African-Americans will not
win the Nobel Prize. But neither will most white people. It never seems to occur to the bigots that we are
all exceptions to these stereotyped rules.

Stacked Cards

Even some whites who recognize that every race has
produced outstanding individuals assume that the

"white race" has more of them than any other race. Ask many Americans to name the ten greatest scientists, writers, and political leaders in the world, and chances are most of the people they name would be white. Some people assume that this proves that whites really are naturally more intelligent and gifted than people of other races. They must have better genes.

In fact, however, there is no reason to believe that racial superiority—or inferiority—has anything to do with it. Chances are that the majority of the names will be male as well as white. Does that mean that men are genetically superior to women? What is more, most of the names would be American. Are Americans genetically superior, too?

The fact is, most Americans see the world from an American perspective. The people we know the most about are Americans. Since the majority of Americans are white, and since whites have dominated American business and politics, it is hardly surprising that most of the prominent people we know about are white. Most Americans know almost nothing about the great men and women of Asia, Africa, Latin America, and the rest of the world.

But, someone might respond, *it does seem that most of the great scientific and economic developments of modern times occurred in the "white" countries of Europe and North America. Doesn't that say something about the white race?*

It is historically true that America and Europe have played the dominant role in world affairs for the past few centuries. A very high percentage of the world's resources and wealth have been concentrated in these mostly white countries during that time. It is virtually inevitable that a high percentage of recent cultural and scientific developments would occur there.

But, *if these white countries have been so dominant, doesn't that prove that whites are naturally superior?* No, it doesn't.

Although Europeans, and their American cousins, have been in the forefront of world affairs for the past few centuries, this has not always been the case. Asians, Africans, Native Americans, and Semitic peoples of the Middle East have all had highly developed civilizations at times in history when the white peoples of the world were relatively backward. Most of the great scientific and cultural developments of those times took place in other lands. They include such great human achievements as the invention of mathematics, the development of written languages, the mining and working of precious metals, and so on.

But what about when all else is equal, as in the United States today? We have lots of people of other races here, and yet most of our outstanding leaders are still white. In the first place, despite the great racial and ethnic mix of our population, 80.3 percent of all Americans are still white.[6] What's more, all else isn't equal. Members of minority groups often start out with enormous social, economic, and educational disadvantages, compared to the typical white American. They also face many more obstacles along the way.

They are more likely than whites to attend a poor school. They are more likely to face prejudice and hostility from fellow students, and perhaps from teachers as well. They are less likely to receive support and encouragement to continue their studies. They are more likely to need to drop out of high school to support themselves. They are more likely to rule out further education as an economic impossibility. And—even after their schooling is completed—they are more likely to face discrimination in the job market.

In short, the cards are stacked against members of minority groups ever getting the chance to reach their full potential—whatever that potential may be.

Self-Stereotyping

Although people usually resent being stereotyped by others, they often stereotype themselves. Going beyond a mere celebration of their group's common heritage, they create a kind of caricature of themselves, and then insist that everyone in their group behave accordingly. Sometimes, like a child who's been falsely accused of stealing so often that he steals something just for spite, they even accept the role the bigots expect them to play.

One of the saddest examples of this self-stereotyping can be seen among some black teenagers today. Teachers and social scientists report that many young black students take it for granted that they will do badly in school. This is particularly true in poor neighborhoods, where expectations for the future tend to be very low.

Worse, some black teenagers consider success in school a betrayal of their race, a sell-out to the white culture. They define black culture as talking a certain way, dressing a certain way—and, most of all, having a certain "black" attitude. This attitude includes disrespect for anything that smacks of white, middle-class values. And, in their eyes, success in school is a white, middle-class value. They consider poor grades and hostility toward teachers, black or white, to be badges of their race. They treat school as a white person's game, and act as though it were somehow more black to fail than to succeed.

These black teenagers ridicule the black students who do well in school. They accuse them of rejecting their racial identity, of being ashamed of the color of their skins. Some inner-city high school students have been beaten up, and even threatened with death, by fellow students, simply because they excelled in school.[7]

Some self-stereotyping young people are just covering up their own insecurity. Jealous that their fellows seem to be smarter than they are, they hide their fear that they might fail in school, even if they tried, behind a mask of rebellion. It's not that I *couldn't* be a good student, they tell themselves. It's just that I don't *want* to be. Why should I? I don't want to be white.

For others, though, self-stereotyping is part of a real attempt to find their own identity, their own cultural values. It seems misguided, however, for them to embrace a cultural value that denies the long African-American tradition of respect for education. This tradition dates back to slave days, when it was against the law in many states to teach black people to read. In those days, slaves and freedmen set up their own underground schools, risking whippings and worse to grab whatever education they could. In the first three-quarters of this century, many black parents worked at several jobs at once to send their sons and daughters to black colleges like Howard and Tuskegee Institute. During the civil-rights movement of the 1950s and '60s, brave black students risked abuse, violence, and sometimes death, just to achieve a decent education in an integrated school.

Now, it seems, the descendants of these same people are turning their backs on the reality of this black experience. They are adopting a negative stereotype for themselves that can only damage their chances for a rewarding life.

Similar self-stereotyping goes on in other minority communities as well. Some Hmong-Americans, for example, pressure their girls to get married young, and to give up thought of further education. Some Native Americans accuse those who leave the reservations of betraying their race and deserting their roots, as though there is only one way for a member of their race to live.

Trees must set down roots, but no tree is made of roots alone. Trees must grow and develop. If Maria Tallchief had stereotyped herself in this way, America would have lost a great ballerina. If Ralph Bunche had stereotyped himself in this way, the world would have lost a Nobel Prize winner.

Whenever people stereotype themselves, they are limiting their own possibilities and cutting off their own futures. This is a sad, and even tragic, thing for someone to do.

Is There Any Truth in the Stereotypes?

Where there's smoke there's fire. Even people who are not especially prejudiced often believe that there must be some truth to racial and ethnic stereotypes.

But, what does it mean that a stereotype is "true"? There's little doubt that you can find examples of individuals of any group who fit the stereotype of that group. But you can also find examples of the same characteristics in people from other groups as well. Any trait that is shared by a high proportion of people in one group is likely to be shared by a high proportion of other people as well.

Many Catholics, for example, probably *are* hypocritical, just as one common anti-Catholic stereotype maintains. But so are many Protestants, Jews, Confucians, Muslims, Buddhists, and many atheists as well. Hypocrisy is a common human failing.

Various groups do have practices and traditions that make them more likely to exhibit certain traits than does the general population. But, even within these groups, the traits are never shared by everyone.

Americans, for whatever reason, have produced

more than their share of modern commercial inventions. In 1989, for instance, Americans received over half the patents issued by the U.S. patent office.[8] Based on that evidence, you could argue that Americans are highly inventive people, just as one positive stereotype claims. But only a very small proportion of Americans have ever earned a patent, and the vast majority of Americans have never invented anything at all.

There are usually fairly obvious reasons why particular traits seem to be more common among one race or ethnic group than among others. It might or might not be so that a relatively high proportion of the Irish become alcoholics. But, even if it were so, it probably would have something to do with the fact that the village "pub" has long been a traditional gathering place for the Irish. There are few other places to get together in Irish villages. But, does this mean that the stereotype that most Irishmen are drunkards is true? No, because the great majority of them are not alcoholics.

One of the most common of all stereotypes is the picture of African-Americans as outstanding athletes. For evidence, people point out that the majority of American professional basketball players are black, even though they make up less than 13 percent of the U.S. population. Many more than 13 percent of the athletes in professional football and baseball are also black, and a high proportion of world-class athletes in various other sports are black as well.

Some people assume this means that blacks are genetically (or biologically) better equipped to be athletes. *They must be, or how could they dominate so many sports?* Yet, the great majority of top-quality hockey players, skiers, swimmers, divers, tennis players, golfers, and athletes in several other sports are white. Why doesn't this mean that whites are naturally better athletes, then?

In reality, there is no proof that blacks (or members of any other race) are biologically better equipped to be athletes. Despite common beliefs, there is no good scientific evidence, for example, that black people are taller than whites, or have longer muscles, or any other genetic (inherited) advantage.

In fact, if racial stereotypes were not so widely accepted, it would seem strange even to ask these questions. "The Swiss and Austrians do very well in World cup skiing," University of Colorado sociology professor Jay Coakley stated to a reporter for USA *Today*. But nobody assumes that they are biologically superior to people from other countries. "Everybody says no wonder they're good skiers. They come from countries with wonderful mountains and they start when they're very young."[9]

If African-Americans make up a higher proportion of professional athletes in certain sports, it might be because more of them work harder at these sports. If whites dominate in skiing and tennis, it might be because more of them have access to mountains and tennis courts.

The image of the superior black athlete can be considered a positive stereotype, because it implies that black people have outstanding physical talents and abilities. But it can also be considered a negative stereotype, because it fits in with the prejudiced idea that black people are more physical, and less intellectual, than whites.

What's the Difference?
Ultimately, the most important question is not whether a stereotype is positive or negative. Or even

whether it is "true." The real question is, what difference does it make?

If I meet a man from Ireland, he might or might not be an alcoholic. I have no good reason to believe he is or is not simply because he comes from there. I don't know of any study that shows how many Irishmen are alcoholics, or how many Norwegians are, either. But, even if it were true that there were three more alcoholics in every hundred Irishmen than in every hundred Norwegians—what difference would that make? How would it change the way I should react toward the Irish in general, or any single Irishman in particular? Or toward Norwegians, for that matter?

All stereotypes are fundamentally dehumanizing. They imply that everyone in a particular group is the same, and that makes it harder to recognize people as individuals. And that is what every person is, no matter what their racial or ethnic background: an individual human being, with his or her own faults and virtues, good qualities and bad. And that is how we should respond to each other.

☞ SOME THINGS TO REMEMBER
Never confuse an individual with a group. The fact that someone belongs to a particular racial, religious, or ethnic group never makes them a bad person. It never makes them a good person, either.

You are not your race. Your race is not you. When Michael Jordan makes an impossible basketball shot, it is his achievement, not the accomplishment of the black race. When James Earl Ray murdered the Rev. Martin Luther King, Jr., it was his crime, not the crime of the white race.

Chapter Six

"YOU'VE GOT TO BE TAUGHT"

In the Rodgers and Hammerstein musical play *South Pacific*, a white American naval officer named Joseph Cable falls in love with a beautiful Pacific island girl. Although he cares for her deeply, he discovers he can't face the prospect of marrying her. How can he take her home to his family in the United States? She is only a native girl. She is not white.

Another character in the play cannot understand Cable's attitude. He demands to know how he could feel this way toward a girl he obviously loves so deeply. Ashamed of his own bigotry, the young American tries to explain that prejudice is something he learned in his youth, from the attitudes of those around him. "You've got to be taught to hate and fear," he sings. "You've got to be carefully taught."

Dr. Howard Erlich, of the National Institute Against Prejudice and Violence, agrees. "Prejudice is learned,"[1] he told *Scholastic Update* magazine. For many of us, the lesson begins at home.

Parents

When we are very young, the world outside the door of our home is a mysterious and exciting place, filled with adventure and danger alike. Most of all, it is filled with strangers—strangers who are fascinating and frightening at the same time.

It is our parents who first introduce us to this wonderful and frightening world outside our door. They are the ones who tell us who these strangers are. They are the ones who tell us which ones we should trust and which we should fear. They are the ones who first explain that "they" are different from "us." Who tell us why "we" are one color, and "they" are some other color. Why "we" go to this church, and "they" go to that church. Why "we" talk so clearly, and "they" have that funny accent.

While we are very young, we tend to assume that our parents are right about everything. When they express hostility toward a racial, religious, or ethnic group, we tend to feel hostile too. When they talk about "niggers," and "spics," and "gringos," and "queers," and "welfare bums," we use those words too. When they tell us that "these people" are good and "those people" are bad, we take their word for it.

Even when something they tell us doesn't sound quite right, we usually accept it. After all, we want our parents to approve of us, and one way to get them to approve of us is to adopt their beliefs—including their prejudices. Often, as Richard W. Brislin, of the Cultural Learning Institute in Hawaii, has pointed out, "Young children develop ... prejudice to please their parents."[2]

Parents don't always teach us their prejudices directly. Or even deliberately. Many parents don't think of themselves as prejudiced at all, and would never want to teach prejudice to their children. They would never dream of using words like "nigger" or "spic." They would never tell their children "blacks are inferior," or "homeless people are all bums." But, as we have seen, everyone has some prejudices. And, unless they try very hard, it is almost impossible for parents not to pass them on to their children, such as

☞ A white mother casts a disapproving look at a group of black teenagers gathered on a street corner.
☞ A black father who is less friendly to white strangers than to strangers of his own race.
☞ Parents of any race who make fun of Jehovah's Witnesses or Seventh Day Adventists who come knocking at the front door.

These parents, and thousands of others, send a subtle message to their children. *There is something wrong with these people*, the message says. *They are not like us.*

But the message isn't only about *them*. It is also about *us*. *We don't like those people*, says the message. *We are better than they are.*

Whether parents intend it or not, children hear these messages both loudly and clearly. By the time they go off to school, they already share the racial beliefs and prejudices of their parents.[3] They already identify with the groups their parents identify with, and feel hostile toward those their parents despise or fear.

When children get older, they usually find that the world is not entirely the way their parents explained it. Eventually, they begin to doubt some of their parents' judgments, and challenge some of their ideas. This is part of the process of growing up.

Among the parental ideas young people question are the racial and ethnic prejudices that have been passed on to them. Yet, even for grown children, the bonds of family prejudice can be hard to break. For parent and child alike, a challenge to the family's racial attitudes can seem like a betrayal. It can seem like siding with the enemy. *How can you defend those people against us?* A citizens' group that works to promote racial tolerance reports that many teenagers "are saying they don't want to be prejudiced, but also don't want to fight with or be alienated from parents who have racist beliefs."[4]

It doesn't always work this way, of course. Parents, like other people, are prejudiced in different degrees. Many try their best not to send prejudiced messages to their children, but to send messages of tolerance, sympathy, and understanding instead. Children of these parents may develop tolerance to please their parents, just as the children of bigots develop bigotry. Other children, meanwhile, reject their parents' bigotry, while others reject their parents' tolerance. Most of us, however, end up accepting many of our parents' prejudices as our own. Too often, we pass them on from generation to generation like some inherited disease.

Peers

"The major influence upon people is people," says D. Bem, in the book *Beliefs, Attitudes, and Human Affairs.*[5] And, after our parents, the people who influence us the most are our peers. Young people bring the prejudices they learn at home with them to the playgrounds, schools, and other places where they gather. There, they teach them to each other.

By the time we reach our midteens, most of us are already learning more of our attitudes from other young people than from our parents.[6] If our friends' prejudices are the same as our parents', the prejudices we've already learned are reinforced. If they are different, we may be drawn away from our parents' attitudes and toward those of our peers.

This is true in many different areas, from social behavior to attitudes toward drugs, sex, and alcohol. But it is particularly true of tribal attitudes. Just as our parents teach us to see ourselves as members of a family, our parents teach us to see ourselves as members of a particular social group. In both cases, that identity can include a racial, ethnic, or religious aspect.

We are white. (Or black. Or Asian. Or whatever.) We are Italian. (Or Chicano. Or Greek. Or whatever.) We are born again Christians. (Or Jews. Or Catholics. Or whatever.) This is what we are. These are our attitudes.

If the people we hang around with when we're young make fun of other races and ethnic groups, we are likely to make fun of them, too. This, we learn, is the way people "like us" behave. If, on the other hand, our social group accepts people of all different backgrounds, we are likely to accept them too.

Even peers we don't know personally can influence our attitudes and behavior. In 1989, this influence was tested on nearly 150 students at the exclusive Smith College in Massachusetts. There had been some racist activities on campus, and students were asked what they thought of them. The questioning was arranged so that each student heard someone who was apparently a fellow student answer first. The "fellow student" was really a plant, however, whose answers were directed by the people giving the test. Those answers had a dramatic effect on the attitudes expressed by the unrehearsed students. Those who heard the "fellow student" give a strongly antiracist answer tended to express strongly antiracist sentiments themselves. Those who heard the supposed "student" express racist beliefs were more likely to express proracist or neutral attitudes.[7]

National Leadership – or the Lack of It

The attitudes, statements, and actions of political and community leaders also affect our own attitudes. This was dramatically demonstrated, in a positive sense, in the 1960s. At the beginning of that decade, racial segregation was still the law in the South, but a growing civil-rights movement had risen to protest it.

By the end of the 1960s, legal segregation had ended. The Jim Crow laws that once enforced racial separation had been struck down by the courts. But it wasn't just laws that had changed during the decade. The attitudes of many white Americans had changed as well. It wasn't just that African-Americans now moved into previously all-white neighborhoods and jobs. In many places (although far from all), they were accepted by whites who would have fought bitterly against their presence only a few years before.

One of the biggest reasons for this change in attitude was the leadership of many national figures, from the justices of the Supreme Court to the presidents John F. Kennedy and Lyndon B. Johnson. They and hundreds of other public officials took strong public stands against racism, and called on the white citizens of the United States to put aside their prejudices. The leaders backed up their words with actions. In addition to laws that protected the rights of black Americans, they provided government legal support and, when necessary, military support as well for black people attempting to exercise those rights.

Bigotry and discrimination did not end with the 1960s, of course. But their effects were greatly reduced. What's more, in every way that can be measured, many of the prejudices that led to them were reduced as well. Interracial alliances and even friendships were established by people who would never have dreamed of becoming close to each other a decade before. By the 1970s, it was no longer socially acceptable to be openly racist. Membership in the Ku Klux Klan and other racist organizations dropped greatly. The number of hate crimes in the country dropped as well.

Unfortunately, moral leadership cuts both ways. Its absence can be as destructive as its presence can be positive. The 1980s and early 1990s saw a resurgence of prejudice and bigotry in America. Hate-group membership rose once again, and the reports of violent hate crimes rose dramatically.[8]

There were many reasons for these unfortunate developments. Economics clearly played a part in them. With American car manufacturers losing badly in competition with Japanese car makers, major cities across the country saw an upsurge in racial incidents directed against Asian-Americans.[9] Well-paying jobs got scarcer and scarcer for middle-class workers in many industries. As competition for the jobs that remained increased, many white people complained of what they called "reverse discrimination." They argued that civil-rights laws, and the fear among employers of lawsuits, gave an unfair advantage to nonwhites and other minorities. They charged that employers often turned down qualified white people for jobs in order to give them to minority job-seekers.

But, some social scientists believe, economic factors were not the only ones fueling the resurgence of prejudice. They say that another reason for the worsening racial tensions was the attitude of some of the nation's most visible political leaders, including the two presidents Ronald Reagan and George Bush. Unlike their predecessors in the 1960s and 1970s, they took few strong public stands against racism. Concentrating on other matters, they seemed to abandon any serious effort to promote increased racial understanding and cooperation in the United States.

It was not that President Reagan and President Bush called for a return to segregation. But, instead of continuing to press white Americans to overcome their prejudices, they acted as though prejudice was no longer a serious problem. Instead of continuing to promote the progress of blacks and other minorities in every aspect of national life, they suggested that perhaps minorities were getting too many advantages under the policies that had been initiated in the 1960s and '70s.

Some critics even accused President Reagan and President Bush of deliberately appealing to racist sentiment in their campaigns for the presidency. Jon Wiener, of the University of California-Irvine, charged that Ronald Reagan frequently "used potent code words, and attacked social programs to legitimize a subtle racism."[10] For example, President Reagan attacked the welfare system by charging that "welfare queens" were using it to cheat American taxpayers. Although he never described the "welfare queens" as black, bigoted voters were bound to picture them that way. When he attacked the Democrats for being soft on "criminals," many voters took it for granted that the criminals he meant were black drug dealers and street criminals.

Critics of the Reagan administration argue that its indifference to prejudice helps explain the rise in racism and intolerance in the 1980s—particularly among young people. As Leonard Zeskind, research director for the Center for Democratic Renewal, explains, "[Today's] kids have come to social consciousness in the age of Reagan, when affirmative action is a bad word and race relations are going backwards."[11]

Young people tend to look up to whomever is president, and to assume that he (and someday, she) represents the mainstream of political thought. When a president regularly complains about programs designed to overcome prejudice, and doesn't suggest any better alternatives, it's not surprising that young people conclude that prejudice is politically respectable.

"I have no doubt," adds Dr. Stuart Cook, a University of Colorado psychiatrist, "that the absence of strong disapproval by our national leaders of racial and ethnic hatreds has found its way into our schools and businesses."[12]

According to some critics, President Bush displayed the same lack of positive leadership as President Reagan. In his 1988 campaign, Democrats accused him of running a campaign commercial that appealed to racist feelings in voters.

The same campaign brought out the anti-ethnic prejudice of some voters. President Bush's Democratic opponent was a Greek-American named Michael Dukakis. Although Bush himself never directly appealed to anti-ethnic sentiment, some of his supporters did. A famous country singer, appearing at a pro-Bush rally, got a big laugh by stumbling over Dukakis's name. It was so foreign-sounding, she complained, that a "real American" could hardly even say it.

In the 1992 campaign, Democrats charged that Bush wasn't just appealing to white racism, he was encouraging it. Democratic candidate Bill Clinton charged the Republicans with wanting to "play the race card." Clinton's fellow Democrat, Paul Tsongas, declared that "Bush [took] the party of Lincoln and turned it into the party of [ex-Nazi and Ku Klux Klan leader] David Duke."[13] Bush had only one campaign strategy, Tsongas stated. That was "to divide and rule."[14]

It wasn't just political opponents who protested the lack of presidential leadership. Fifty-seven percent of the readers and opinion leaders asked by *USA Week-*

end magazine to say who was doing the "least effective job of protecting civil rights" in 1991, picked President Bush.[15]

Even some of their critics admitted that leaders like Reagan and Bush might not have been bigots themselves. They might not have always realized what "code words" like "welfare queens" would mean to many voters. But leaders do not have to be active bigots themselves to promote bigotry in others. These presidents' lack of positive leadership in racial matters helped to make bigotry socially acceptable again. Their silence allowed the bigots to assume that they were on the bigots' side.

Wartime Propaganda

Most of the time, the mainstream American media do their best to promote racial goodwill and understanding. But, in times of war, they often join with the government to drum up hatred against the enemy. This hatred is often directed toward the people of the enemy nation, and sometimes even to Americans descended from them.

Whatever nationality the enemy happens to be is stereotyped and demonized. Everything is done to keep the public from thinking of citizens of the enemy country as individual human beings. Instead, they are presented as evil stereotypes, totally lacking in ordinary human qualities.

In World War II, for example, all the Germans became Nazi *beasts*, and the Japanese became *little yellow devils*. In Korea, the North Koreans and Communist Chinese were *the yellow horde*. Many of the same kinds of things are said about all enemies, whoever they are. *They're not like us. They don't have the same feelings we do. They have no respect for human life.*

Reports of enemy atrocities are reported with

little questioning. Later on, most, if not all of these reports, turn out to be false. During World War I, for example, there were frequent reports that German troops were gleefully bayoneting Belgian babies, although nothing like that actually seems to have occurred.

During World War II, press and public officials alike tended to refer to the enemy by racial slurs. The banner headline with which the New York Daily News announced the Japanese attack on Pearl Harbor read "JAPS BOMB HAWAII." Slurs like "Jap" and "kraut" were the commonly accepted terms Americans used for the people of Japan and Germany.

Although some German and Italian-Americans suffered from war-inspired prejudice during World War II, it was the Japanese-Americans who suffered most. The Democratic administration of President Franklin D. Roosevelt imprisoned thousands of them in internment camps, where they were held until the war was over. Whole families, including old women and infants, were imprisoned on the grounds that people of Japanese ancestry represented a security threat to the nation.

This seemed reasonable to most white Americans at the time. After all, Americans were dying fighting Japanese soldiers abroad. It seemed foolhardy to let possible Japanese agents live freely inside the country. But this logic was laced with racial prejudice. It ignored the fact that the people in the internment camps were *not* Japanese, except by race. They were Americans.

What's more, the United States was also at war with Germany and Italy at the time, and there was no mass imprisonment of German-Americans or Italian-Americans. In fact, there was more reason to imprison German-Americans than Japanese-Americans. Many German-Americans had belonged to the several pro-

Nazi organizations that operated in the United States before the war. And some German Americans had, in fact, supported the Germans during World War I. Meanwhile, no Japanese-American was ever convicted of betraying America. And yet, German-Americans and Italian-Americans were assumed to be loyal, while Japanese-Americans were not—purely because of their race.

During more recent wars, U.S. government officials have tried to distance themselves from the kind of overt racism expressed by terms like "kraut" and "Jap." During the war with Iraq, for example, President Bush frequently repeated that his—and America's—quarrel was not with the Arab people of Iraq, only with that nation's government.

Nonetheless, prejudice against Arabs surged during Desert Storm. There were at least one hundred incidents of verbal harassment of Arabs (or people who seemed to be Arabs) reported in Washington, D.C., alone during the short war.[16] Elsewhere, several Arab-American-owned businesses were burned.

Things got so bad in some cities that police advised Arab-Americans to "low-key their heritage." Not surprisingly, many Arab-Americans were offended to get such shocking advice from public officials.[17]

Community Leaders and Rabble-Rousers

Every racial and ethnic community seems to have its own rabble-rousers: leaders and would-be leaders who stir up hatred of other ethnic groups. The white community has its white supremacists. Representatives of organizations like the Ku Klux Klan, the "Christian Identity" movement, and the White Aryan Resistance stir up ethnic and religious hatreds around the country. And recruiters for the Klan, neo-Nazi groups, and the skinheads prey particularly on high school and college students, trying to inject them with their poison.

But minority communities have their own hate mongers, who inflame hostility toward other minorities and the majority alike. Whatever is wrong with the community is "their" fault. "They" are destroying "us." What's more, these leaders insist, they are doing it *on purpose*. Very often, they claim some kind of conspiracy. *Drugs are a white plot to destroy the black communities. AIDS is a government plot to kill off all black people. Whites are adopting Native American babies in order to wipe out the Indian race.*

Anti-semitism is as strong among minority hate mongers as it is among white supremacists. They, too, scapegoat Jews, presenting them as demonic villains who control the world's money supply, and use it to keep other minorities in bondage.

Some hate mongers may actually believe their conspiracy theories. But, for others, inciting anger and hatred toward outsiders is mostly a way to unify their followers, and to confirm their own position of leadership. *I am the one who will reveal the conspirators to you. I am the one who will lead "us" in the fight against "them."*

Whether individual hate mongers are sincere or not, belief in such conspiracies distracts from the very real evils of discrimination, racist social institutions, and the prejudices that underpin them. Bigotry is not the solution to bigotry. Prejudice is not going to overturn prejudice. And, when a black leader like Minister Louis Farrakhan attacks Jews and calls Judaism a "gutter religion," he is stirring up prejudice as surely as a Ku Klux Klan wizard who rails against "nigras on welfare."

Stereotypes in the Media

Many of the images of minority life seen in the movies and on TV are downbeat, and fit in all too well with the negative stereotypes of those groups. Seventy-four percent of newsmakers polled for *USA Weekend* in 1991 said that media coverage of African-Americans was too negative. A big majority also thought that coverage of Hispanics (70 percent) and Native Americans (69 percent) was too negative as well.[18]

News stories that deal with minorities are nearly always concerned with the dark side of life: crime in the cities, poverty, prisons, drugs, illegal immigration, and so on. There are relatively few upbeat stories featuring middle-class minority people who are living successful and productive lives. The few exceptions tend to deal with the more colorful or "exotic" aspects of minority life—rap music, for example, or a celebration of the Chinese New Year. "The only news you get [about] Hispanic people and lands," one Hispanic-American complains, are those that involve "earthquakes, bullfighting, and coups d'etats."[19]

The overwhelming majority of leading roles in the movies and on TV are played by white actors, whether male or female. This is particularly true of roles that are seen as heroic, and those that portray people who are exceptionally successful in life. Minority actors are most often seen playing minor roles, often as drug addicts, prostitutes, criminals, or crime victims. Their characters are rarely presented as complex human beings who share the same ordinary problems and concerns that mainstream white Americans do.

The media stereotyping of minorities is rarely deliberate. Nor is it done out of malice. If anything, television and movie producers, directors, and writers are more protolerance than the public at large. In fact, even some of the most negative media portrayals of minorities are intended to be sympathetic. After all, the producers would argue, it is only by showing the terrible results of prejudice and discrimination that social change can be encouraged.

The majority of leading roles are given to white actors simply because the majority of the American audience is white. The producers believe that they are more interested in seeing white actors than in seeing actors of other races. As to why so many villains are portrayed as members of racial minorities, the makers of entertainment programs are as subject to thinking in stereotypes as anyone else.

Where news is concerned, the fact that so many minority-related stories are downbeat is partly explained by the nature of news itself. News tends to be defined mostly as what's-gone-wrong-today, so most news stories involving people of any race or ethnic group are downbeat. Because certain minorities are so heavily identified with social problems, from poverty to discrimination, this is even more true for minorities.

Whatever the reasons for the heavily downbeat portrayal of minorities in the media, it tends to reinforce negative stereotypes. And that, in turn, reinforces prejudice against them.

☞   SOMETHING TO REMEMBER

Just as the past influences the present, your background influences you. You were raised in a certain way. You have learned certain things from your family, your teachers, and your religious leaders. You have shared certain experiences with those around you. You cannot help being influenced by your past, and by the thoughts, feelings, and prejudices of those around you. But this does not mean that you have to surrender yourself to these influences. Nor does it mean that you have to think the way your parents think, or the way your friends think, or the way anyone else thinks. The final responsibility for your opinions—and your prejudices—is yours.

Chapter Seven
WHAT'S SO BAD ABOUT PREJUDICE, ANYWAY?

What's so bad about a little prejudice, anyway? Everybody's prejudiced, aren't they? How bad can it be? So what if I don't like Jews? Or Catholics? So what if I call Latinos "spics," Arabs "camel-jockeys," and homosexuals "queers"? So what if I don't want any of them living next door to me? What does it really matter?

The fact is, it matters a lot. Prejudice is morally wrong, according to all the major religions. It is psychologically harmful to its victims and to the bigots alike. And it is enormously destructive to society as a whole.

Economic and Health Effects

Some of the effects of prejudice, and the discrimination that follows from it, can be deduced from the statistics that compare certain minority groups to the rest of the American population. Despite some white Americans' impression that minorities get all the economic breaks, many minority groups are still seriously disadvantaged. One-third of all African-Americans are poor, including fully half of all black children. The percentage of unemployed African-Americans looking for work is twice that of whites. Those who do find work earn, on average, only 60 percent of what whites do.[1] And finally, the average African-American dies more than seven years earlier than the average white American.[2]

One-fourth of all Native Americans live in poverty, and one-third die before they are forty-five years old.[3]

The comparisons at every age tell the story. Twice as many black babies die as white babies, and one-and-one-half times as many Native American babies.

The death rates for adults from twenty-five to forty-five years of age are just as alarming. Two-and-a-half times as many black Americans die at these ages as whites, 1.8 times as many Native Americans, and 1.25 as many Hispanics.[4]

Native American teenagers are twice as likely to die by violence as white teenagers.[5] Black teenagers are seven times as likely to be murdered. Native American and Hispanic teens three times as likely.[6]

Prejudice is not the only reason for these shocking realities, but it contributes to all of them. It is no accident that the most discriminated-against minorities are at the bottom of the health and economic ladders.

Destroying Self-Esteem

Many of the worst effects of prejudice don't show up in numbers. They are internal. They work their damage inside the minds, hearts, and spirits of the victims and the bigots alike.

Ironically, the self-hatred that leads people like David Cevette to become bigots produces a similar self-hatred in the victims of this prejudice as well. "It is inevitable," writes Edith Folb, of San Francisco State University, "that nondominant peoples will experience, indeed be subjected to ... varying degrees of fear, denial, and self-hatred."[7]

Being continually abused or ignored, patronized

or discriminated against, eats away at a person's self-esteem. People who are continually told that they are inferior, or unworthy, often come to believe it themselves.

Children who are physically or emotionally abused frequently come to believe that they deserve their ill-treatment. They may protest, they may scream or cry, but deep down inside they feel there must be something wrong with them. They must be bad. Otherwise, why would they be treated this way? Something similar happens with victims of discrimination. Finding themselves at the bottom of the social and economic heap, they begin to doubt their own abilities. Regarded as second-class citizens by society, they begin to feel that their fellow citizens may be right. Maybe they deserve to be where they are. Maybe there is something wrong with them.

In one revealing survey of adults in the Chicago area, 14 percent of the African-Americans polled agreed with the statement that blacks have "less inborn ability to learn than whites." Only 9 percent of the whites polled agreed with the same statement.[8] This means that more of the African-Americans surveyed had come to believe the negative stereotype about them than had the whites. In that sense, they had become more prejudiced against their own race than whites were. There could hardly be a sadder demonstration of the ability of prejudice to undermine the self-esteem of its victims.

A whole branch of the cosmetic industry has developed to provide African-Americans with hair straighteners, skin-lightening creams, and other products that will help them look more like white people. Some black people even have their skins partly peeled off with chemicals, in the hope that the layers underneath will be less dark.[9]

Why would people want to do these things? One answer is that the majority white culture sets the standards for beauty in America, and many people who use the above products are simply trying to live up to it. But another, more depressing answer was suggested by a young African-American woman who told the *Maury Povich* television show, "I don't like who I am." Some of her fellow African-Americans in the audience accused her of wanting to be white, but under further questioning by the host, it became clear that it wasn't so much that she wanted to be *white*. She just didn't want to be *black* anymore. She found it too painful being black in America.

Her pain, and the pain of many other blacks, Asian-Americans, Native Americans, and others who wish they could blend into white society is understandable. Since life is so much easier for those who do not face the prejudice of the majority every day, who can blame someone for wishing to join them?

And yet, their rejection of their ethnic identity is, to some extent, a rejection of themselves. At the very least, this is psychologically unhealthy. What's more, it angers many of their fellows who see the rejection as a betrayal of their people. The anger and guilt of both sides in the argument feed each other, and the self-esteem of the whole group suffers.

Violence

Self-rejection is tragic. It is also dangerous. As Eddie Brown, an officer in a group of black businessmen in Milwaukee, Wisconsin, explains: "Institutional racism and segregation, together with internalized racism, self-hatred and a lack of knowledge about oneself [manifests] itself into violence."[10]

The violence takes many forms. A high level of drug use. Suicide. And, most dramatically, the explosion of violent crime that has occurred in many inner-city ghettos, Indian reservations, barrios, and other ethnic neighborhoods around the country.

At least thirty-four major American cities set new murder records in 1991, the latest year for which there are statistics.[11] A high proportion of the killings took place within the minority communities. "Self-hate leads people to engage in destructive acts, both inward and outward. They are striking out against the weakest link in the chain, which is usually people who look like them," says Professor Earnest Spaights, University of Wisconsin-Milwaukee.[12]

At first, it might seem that the slaughter in the neighborhoods has little or nothing to do with the majority community. *It's their problem. What do we care if they want to kill each other off?* But, ultimately, the growing violence affects not just its immediate victims, but everyone in society. It leads directly to an increasing breakdown in the quality of life.

People in many big cities live in fear. They are afraid to walk in certain neighborhoods at night, or to ride the subways even in the daytime. They feel a sense of relief when they enter their homes, as though they have escaped from something. They live behind barred windows and double- and triple-locked doors, as though they were prisoners.

Prisoners in Our Own Minds

Prejudice imprisons people in more ways than one. We define ourselves as being different from each other, and then dislike, distrust, and fear one another, based on those definitions. In this way, we create our own enemies, and then build a fortress of hostility and bias to protect us from those enemies. The stronger our prejudices, the bigger the fortress.

The walls of this fortress are built to keep others

out. To keep *us* safe from *them*. But every wall has two sides. The same wall that keeps you out keeps me in. For the bigot, then, the walls of prejudice make a prison as well as a fort against others.

Like other prisoners, bigots find it hard to relate to the real world outside. They cannot even envision that world very clearly. They see everything through the heavy fog of their own preconceptions and hostility. When that fog becomes thick enough, the bigot finds it hard to see reality at all. This may or may not result in problems for the victims of the bigot's prejudice, but it inevitably causes problems for the bigot herself or himself. "[F]lawed perceptions," as one psychology textbook pointed out, "damage our relationships and consequently, our personal adjustment."[13]

Hate Crimes

"The most disturbing thing about hate," said ex-President Jimmy Carter, "is that all of us have it in us."[14]

Hatred is more than simple dislike, and even more than anger. It is a deep desire to hurt, to do damage to the person or group you hate. And it is often prejudice that allows this hate to form and sometimes to explode.

The number of hate crimes—crimes motivated by racial, religious, ethnic, or other bias—rose throughout the 1980s. "The level of bigoted violence has reached epidemic levels in America," declared an antihate activist in 1990.[15] Thirty states have responded by passing laws that add extra penalties for crimes committed out of racial or other prejudice.[16]

"Society is saying this kind of criminal act is more serious and worthy of harsher punishment because of the bigoted motive," explains Steven Freeman, direc-

tor of legal affairs with the Anti-Defamation League of
B'nai B'rith. "These ... crimes impact not only the
individual victim but also other members of the victim's community and the community as a whole."[17]

Yet, all over the country Americans are still being
attacked, beaten, and even killed by other Americans
simply because they are black. Or brown. Or yellow.
Or Jewish. Or homeless. Or homosexual. Or because
they seem to be one of these things.

The Threat to the Economy

The effects of prejudice on the American economy are
less obvious than some of the other effects discussed
here. But they are just as real. The people of any
country make up one of its most valuable resources.
They are what develop its culture, found its industries,
grow its food, and manufacture and transport its
goods. In short, they are the ones who make the country's economy work.

As long as America has large numbers of people
who are uneducated, poor, and unhealthy, it will never
be able to achieve its full economic potential. The
uneducated cannot work at the skilled jobs needed to
make a modern economy prosper. The poor cannot
afford to consume the products the economy produces. And the unhealthy are a constant drain on
badly needed economic and medical resources.

To the extent that prejudice and discrimination
help to keep millions of Americans in those conditions, they are damaging the American economy. As
the ex-Senator Paul Tsongas declared during his campaign for the Democratic presidential nomination in
1992: "To discriminate against anyone, for whatever
reason, gives you a lesser country. It makes you less
able to compete."[18]

For a time, when our economy was by far the

richest and most powerful in the world, it seemed that we could afford our prejudices. But that's no longer true. The increasingly strong competition from Japan, Europe, and other places now presents an enormous challenge to our economy. We will need all our human resources to meet that challenge. As Senator Bill Bradley (Dem.-NJ) has said, "We will never win the global economic race if we have to carry the burden of an increasingly larger unskilled population."[19]

☞ SOMETHING TO REMEMBER

All prejudices are wrong, but not all prejudices are equal. No racial or ethnic group should be prejudiced against any other. No person should be prejudiced against anyone. In the long run, every prejudice hurts those who feel it. But some prejudices are more socially and economically destructive than others. Because the white majority is the most socially and economically powerful group in the country, their prejudices tend to be the most destructive of all.

Chapter Eight
WORKING TO OVERCOME
OUR PREJUDICES

Understanding prejudice is not enough. We must do our best to overcome it, both in ourselves and in society at large.

The fight to overcome prejudice begins in our own minds and hearts. It begins with recognizing our own prejudices for what they are, and examining them as coolly and objectively as we can.

Examining Our Prejudices
Whenever we find ourselves disliking a person who belongs to a different group than we do, or feeling uncomfortable around her or him, we should ask ourselves why we feel this way. What is it about the person that makes me nervous, or angry? Is he a bully? Is she dishonest? Did he or she do something unpleasant, immoral, or cruel? If so, perhaps we are justified in disliking them. If not, we have to look deeper into our own feelings.

When we really examine our negative feelings about someone, we sometimes find that they don't stem from anything that person did, but from the racial, religious, or ethnic group to which they belong. In such cases, we need to understand that the problem is ours, not theirs. Something in ourselves is too insecure to accept ethnic differences. This is a flaw in us, and we must learn to overcome it, or risk becoming sickened by the disease of bigotry.

Even when we find that we are justified in disliking certain individuals who belong to a group, that doesn't justify us in disliking the entire group. No matter what the individuals have done to justify our hostility, *they* are the ones who did it, not the others in their group. We must beware of generalizing our dislikes—of expanding a personal dislike of one or two people to include a whole group.

Accepting Our Own Cultural Identity

Whenever you feel a strong dislike of people of another race, religion, or ethnic group, chances are that you also feel uncomfortable about yourself in some way. Just as there is a high correlation between prejudice and low self-esteem, there is a high correlation between high self-esteem and tolerance of those who are different. In other words, the better you feel about yourself, the better you're likely to feel about other people.

One important key to becoming more comfortable with yourself is coming to terms with your own ethnic identity. While most of us take some pride in our heritage, many of us also feel a little uncomfortable about it, or consider it a burden in some way. "Everyone has [both] positive and negative feelings about their background," says Joe Giordano, of the Proud to be Me program in Sarasota.[1]

Some sensitive members of the majority feel guilty for the discrimination and racism that have kept them at the top of the social ladder for so long. Many members of minorities, on the other hand, feel that their racial or ethnic background holds them back and makes them second-class citizens. If people like these want to feel truly comfortable with themselves, they need to learn to accept—and even celebrate—their ethnicity, whatever it may be.

It is useful to know the history of your ethnic group: to learn about its struggles, its sacrifices, and its accomplishments. This is important for everyone, but it is particularly important for minority young people. Almost everyone is familiar with the achievements of distinguished white Americans and Europeans, past and present. Their accomplishments are highly publicized in the mainstream culture. But the accomplishments of distinguished members of minority groups are often ignored.

Fabu Mogaka, a consultant on African-American culture, argues that young minority people must learn to affirm their own identities. But, before they can do that, they have to learn about the history and accomplishments of others, past and present, who belong to the same racial or ethnic group. "When you [look] at your own history," she tells young people, "it will always give you examples of people who struggled— against poverty, against racism."[2]

The point is not to take some kind of phony credit for what others in your ethnic or racial group have done. It is simply to realize that people who share your ethnic or racial identity have proven themselves to be every bit as noble and able as members of any other group. Knowing that they have accomplished great things can help you know that you could accomplish them too.

Accepting your ethnicity is important, but it is just as important not to overemphasize it. Your ethnicity is not *you*. It is just one thing *about* you. Many other things go into your personal identity. Many other factors play parts in making you what you are. Your

family, your neighborhood, your community, your
school, your friends, the movies and television programs you watch, the things you read, and most of all
your individual character and personality—all these
are at least as important as your ethnicity in determin-
ing who you are.

And what is true of you is true of everyone else
as well. Their ethnicity is just one part of what they
are, but not the most important part.

Taking the Bad with the Good

Not everything about your heritage is positive. There
is much to be proud of, but also much to be ashamed
of, in the history of every race and culture. People of
every creed and ethnic group have done great things,
but they have also committed terrible crimes.

It is important for African-Americans to know that
black Africans participated in the slave trade, just as
it is important for white Americans to realize that
their forebears did the same. It is important for Native
Americans to know that some early American tribes
carried out near genocide against other tribes, just as
it is important for white Americans to know that their
ancestors did the same. It is important for white people to realize that the most horrendous crimes of the
twentieth century—the Nazi holocaust in Europe and
the massive suffering caused by Stalinization in the
Soviet Union—were committed by white people.

Why do we need to know these bad things about
our ethnic backgrounds? Because knowing them helps
us to put our ethnicity in perspective. It makes us
vividly aware that no race or ethnic group has a mo-
nopoly on goodness, or on evil either. All have suffered, and all have inflicted suffering on others. When
we accept our own groups' faults and weaknesses, we
will find it easier to accept those of other people.

Accepting Cultural Differences

Part of accepting our own cultural and ethnic identity is recognizing real differences between our group and others. Different ethnic groups have different customs, habits, and traditions. The United States would be a much duller and poorer place if they didn't.

Where would we be without jazz and rap music, both of which have roots in African-American culture? Where would we be without Santa Claus, the exchanging of gifts at Christmas, and New Year's celebrations, all of which have roots in central-European traditions? Where would we be without German beer? Swiss cheese? Chinese, Mexican, and Italian cooking? Or any of the thousands of other contributions various ethnic groups have made to our American culture?

But people from different backgrounds will also have different attitudes about some things. These different attitudes can easily lead to misunderstandings and bad feelings. Most Americans, for example, consider it polite to smile at strangers. But other people, particularly those with Middle Eastern and Asian backgrounds, consider it rude. Because of this difference, immigrants from these countries sometimes assume that native-born Americans are very boorish, while many native-born Americans consider the newcomers unfriendly.

North Americans tend to like more physical space around them than do people from Latin America. Given a choice, most non-Latin Americans prefer to stand two feet or more away from someone they're talking with. A Latin American, on the other hand, is apt to stand much closer. Two social scientists report watching a conversation take place between a North American and a Latin American in a long hallway. The Latin American kept edging a little closer to his companion, while the North American kept edging a little farther away. They longer they talked, the farther down the hallway they moved. By the time the conversation was over, the two men had moved forty feet from one end of the hall to the other![3]

Most cultural differences like these are insignificant, but the misunderstandings that result from them are not. Very often, much of the discomfort we feel around people from other ethnic backgrounds results from just such little differences as these. The problem comes when we don't recognize the differences for what they are. Instead, we assume our uneasiness flows from some deeper or more sinister cause.

Instead of simply understanding that the Latin American likes to stand closer to a person, the North American might feel *he's trying to bully me*. Instead of simply realizing that the North American is more comfortable standing farther apart, the Latin American might feel, He *doesn't like me*. He might even think, He *must be prejudiced against Hispanics*.

Instead of merely recognizing other people's behaviors as different, we think of them as "wrong." We assume they indicate some fault in the other person's character. But the more we recognize cultural differences for what they really are, the less we will be misled by them. The less we will misunderstand each other, and the less discomfort and hostility we will feel.

Seeking Out Common Experiences

Ultimately, we all have much more in common than we have that sets us apart. We all have the same basic needs for food, shelter, clothing, and human companionship. We all have the same basic fears and desires. We all laugh, and cry, and have the capacity for love and hate. We all suffer. We all die.

The more we recognize how much we share as

human beings, the less likely we will be to be led astray by prejudice. In order to help us recognize our similarities, it helps to seek out common experiences: to join clubs, study groups, sports teams, and other organizations that will bring us in contact with people who might come from different backgrounds, but who have some of the same interests that we do.

Sharing experiences with others can help us understand and appreciate each other. At the very least, it teaches us that all Jews, or blacks, or Hispanics, or white people—or members of any other group—are not alike. They are individuals, just as we are.

Understanding Our Fears

Much modern prejudice is rooted in physical fear. At some times, and in some places, fear of people from another race or ethnic group is almost unavoidable. In certain southern towns during the 1960s, for example, small groups of white people often attacked black people at random, out of anger at what the civil-rights movement was doing. Under those circumstances, it was hard for any African-American walking alone at night not to regard any crowd of unknown white people with suspicion. In some racially troubled high schools today, violence frequently occurs along racial lines. In a school where ethnic or racial gangs have been known to attack students from other backgrounds, it is hard for any student not to regard unknown groups with anxiety. In situations like these, a certain amount of wariness is only practical. Unfortunately, this sensible suspicion often feeds racial and ethnic prejudice.

It is vital to keep our fears in perspective. Certainly, there are dangerous people in the world. Certainly, there are dangerous neighborhoods. But, for most Americans, the world outside our doors is not really as threatening as it might seem. It is important for each of us to understand the reality of our own situation. We should not be foolhardy or put ourselves in pointless danger. But, at the same time, we must not live in such unrealistic fear that we become too paralyzed to live full and productive lives. Nor should we become hostile toward the people with whom we share American society and the world.

The great majority of Americans will never be the victim of a violent crime of any kind. Of those who will, most will be victimized by members of their own race. Despite widespread belief, a white person is much more likely to be victimized by another white person than by a criminal of any other color. By the same token, African-Americans are more likely to fall victim to black criminals than to white ones. The same is true of Native Americans, Asians, and other ethnic groups. What's more, 54 percent of all murder victims aren't killed by strangers of any race, but by someone they know personally—often a member of their own family.[4]

Understanding these realities can help make sure that our fear of crime will not become twisted into a general fear of people of other races. We must always remember that it is not black people we have reason to fear. Or white people. Or people of any other color. It is violent people.

The Illusion of Superiority

When we examine our racial and ethnic prejudices closely enough, we realize that they are based on two false ideas. One: *We are different than they are.* Two: *We are better than they are.*

But what do these ideas really mean? How are we "different"? How are we "better"? What happens when we break these questions down, so that they can be asked in more meaningful ways? Is everyone in our group better looking than those in other groups? Are we stronger? Are we smarter? Or what?

Once the question is broken down, the answer almost always is: some of us are better (in this specific way) than some of them. But some of them are also better (in this specific way) than some of us. In other words, there is no truth to the general statement that *we are better than they are.*

Most of us rarely examine our prejudices in this way. Most of us never examine our prejudices at all. We simply follow them blindly. Once we do start to examine our prejudices, however, they usually collapse.

☞ SOME THINGS TO REMEMBER
Having prejudices doesn't make you a bad person. Everyone has prejudices. The challenge is to overcome those prejudices, and move beyond them.

Before you judge other people—whatever their skin color or cultural background—try to put yourself in their place. Try to imagine what they must be feeling, and why. Expect—and accept—cultural differences.

Chapter Nine
OVERCOMING DESPAIR

Dealing with your own prejudices is one thing. Dealing with the prejudices of other people—and particularly their prejudices against you—is something else again.

In the next chapter, we will explore some ways in which all of us, whatever our race, creed, or color, can work to overcome the prejudices in society at large. But what about those of us who bear the brunt of discrimination?

How can young African-Americans, Hispanics, and members of other minorities convince people not to see them as stereotypes? Not to look down on them, underestimate them, hate them, or discriminate against them because of their racial, religious, or ethnic group?

In most cases, they can't.

What they can do, however, is prepare themselves to succeed in life despite the barriers that bigotry and institutional racism will place in their way.

The Message of Despair
Of all those barriers, the most difficult to climb over is despair—the temptation to give up before you start.

Ironically, the sense of hopelessness many young people feel is partly fueled by the battle against discrimination itself. Many community and civil-rights leaders focus their efforts on trying to get the majority society to change. They speak with great eloquence about the many injustices their people face, hammering away at the need for society to do something about them.

This is a good and necessary demand. Without it, how can the barriers ever be broken down? How can society be forced to change? The social evils these leaders complain about are real, and society must change. But, by constantly dwelling on the difficulties minorities face, community leaders sometimes send unfortunate messages to the young.

It's all society's fault, proclaims one of these messages. *We are not responsible for anything we do. If one of us commits a crime—or takes drugs, or beats our spouse, or children—it's not their fault. It's what society is doing to us.* This attitude underlies the outrage that members of some minority groups feel whenever prominent members of their group are charged with serious crimes. It is an outrage directed not against the apparent criminals, but against society for bringing the criminals to trial. Many African-Americans even protested the imprisonment of Washington, D.C., mayor Marion Barry, and heavyweight boxer Mike Tyson, although both were very powerful and privileged members of society, convicted after apparently fair trials. *We must always stick up for one of our own. It doesn't matter if they are guilty or not. Even if they did it, it's not their fault. It's society's fault.*

This can be a damaging message for young people to hear, and a crippling one for them to believe. If it's not Marion Barry's fault, or Mike Tyson's fault, then it's not their fault, either. *Society's the thing that's got to change. Not you. There's nothing you can do. The game is stacked against you. You can't win.* And, too often, this message echoes in their heads, *Why try?*

Some young minority members hear the message

of despair all too clearly. They believe it because it fits in so well with what they experience in their lives: the poverty, crime, and adult hopelessness they see around them. But that message puts them at an even greater disadvantage.

Clarence Thomas, the second black man in history to sit on the United States Supreme Court, surprised a 1985 college commencement class by telling them that he had "had an advantage over black students and kids today." It was a surprising statement from a man who grew up in the South in the days of legal segregation. When Thomas was a boy, a black child would have been considered crazy to dream of sitting on a state appeals court, much less the Supreme Court of the United States. What advantage did Thomas mean?

"I had never heard any excuses made," he explained. The hard-working black men he saw around him in his youth knew they would never make as much money as whites who didn't work half as hard. The black women knew they could never be anything but maids and cooks in white people's houses. What's more, they "knew it was prejudice which caused their plight, but that didn't stop them from working. . . . They weren't pinned down by it." And they never gave up. "They fought discrimination."

Black students today, Thomas said, "have a much tougher road. You now have a popular national rhetoric which says that you can't learn because of racism, you can't get up in the morning because of racism. Unlike me, you must not only overcome the repressiveness of racism, you must also overcome the lure of excuses. You have twice the job I had."[1]

Too many young people give in to the tempting lure of excuses. They give up. They drop out of school. They get jobs that pay a minimum wage or less, and don't look for anything better. Or they go on public assistance because they can't get even that kind of job. Young girls get pregnant. Young boys get girls pregnant, and often desert them. Many take drugs, or start to drink too much. Some turn to crime. They rob grocery stores, or they deal drugs. They don't see any choice.

But there is a choice.

Another Message

It is vital that today's young people—and particularly poor, minority young people—know that the message of despair is false. It is vital for them to know that, even stacked against them, the game can still be won. A decent life can still be had. This is proven by the fact that, despite the sometimes terrible odds, millions of black, Hispanic, Native American, and other minority people live such lives today.

Today's young people need to hear another message, like the one delivered by Fabu Mogaka, a consultant on African-American culture. "[W]e know that racism is real," Ms. Mogaka says. "And we know the harm that it does. But you can't let [racism] control your life."[2]

Drew Brown, the first African-American flying ace, has another message as well. He tells minority teenagers that the key to overcoming the odds against them is getting an education. And he doesn't mean just a high school education. With a college education, he says you will be putting yourself in a position to get a good job, raise a strong family, and build financial security. Without it, you will be making it almost impossible for any of these things to happen.[3]

Young people aren't the only ones who need to hear these messages. Parents need to hear them too. Some minority parents are so filled with pain and sympathy for their children's plight, that they demand very little of them. So aware of the obstacles their children face in life, they haven't the heart to press them to do well in school. *What's the point?* they feel. *The school's no good, anyway. The teachers don't care. Besides, as poor as we are, how can my daughter ever hope to get to college? Coming from this barrio (or this ghetto, or this reservation), how can my son ever compete for a decent job with the white kids from the good neighborhoods?*

And it's not just the parents. Too many teachers also demand little from poor minority students, while their friends often press them *not* to excel. With all these forces promising them that they will fail, it's not surprising that so many don't even try.

But the fact is that a significant proportion of those who give up could succeed if they did try. And many do. Millions of parents and children refuse to give in to hopelessness and despair. And for them, there is often a way—in spite of racism, and even in spite of poverty. Minority young people who stay in school, who work hard at their studies, and who do well at them can often find a way to get into college, or a good job-training program of some kind.

If college is their goal, students or their parents should talk to their school advisers as early in their educational careers as possible. In addition, they should talk to the admissions people in their local colleges and universities. If a student is told that she is not qualified, she should ask what she needs to do to get qualified. And then do it.

It will probably not be easy. For some students, it might prove to be impossible. The cards are still stacked against minorities in this country—and against poor minorities most of all. Many will fail, but many will succeed.

It is important to understand that the odds are

no longer as bad as they once were. For those who stay in school, and learn, the odds are probably better now than they have ever been. As Peter Brown of Scripps-Howard Newspapers told the National Press Club Symposium on Race Relations and Politics, "All the data shows ... increasing acceptance of blacks in this country."[4] The same is true for most other minorities.

What is more, recent college outreach programs, affirmative-action policies, and other factors mean that more minority students are able to go to college than ever before. In 1990, almost one-third of all black high school graduates went on to college.[5]

☞   SOME THINGS TO REMEMBER

It is not fair that some of us start out with so many disadvantages. It is not fair that some of us have to overcome the extra barriers of prejudice and discrimination at every step along our way. But that is the reality in America today. And, as long as it is, minority young people will have to work harder, and fight harder, to get what they want out of life.

It is important to recognize the barriers that society erects against members of minority groups. But it is also important to measure them accurately. If a young person sees those barriers as higher or stronger than they really are, he or she will be discouraged from ever attempting to leap over them—much less to tear them down.

Chapter Ten

WORKING TO OVERCOME
THE PREJUDICES
OF OTHERS

Fortunately, there are many things we can do to help reduce the level of prejudice in America today. Some of the measures discussed in this chapter might seem small and insignificant. Certainly, none of them are going to wipe out prejudice or end discrimination altogether. But, taken together, actions like these can make a real difference. They can help to make racism and other prejudices unacceptable, once again, in American society.

Be Careful What You Say

Whether you like it or not, you are an example to your friends and acquaintances. What you do counts—and so does what you say.

The old childhood saying "Sticks and stones may break my bones, but words will never hurt me" is nonsense. Words *can* hurt. *Nigger. Spook. Beaner. Spic. Squaw. Breed. Hebe. Kike. Gook. Slant.* Words like these can hurt a lot.

Ethnic epithets and racial slurs are not just insulting to individuals, they are insulting to everyone who belongs to the same racial, ethnic, or religious group.

It's sometimes hard for people to understand how much a word like "nigger" can hurt, particularly for young white people. *After all, they're just words, aren't they? You hear them all the time. In the school yard. In the movies. On TV. Even at home. A lot of people who use them don't mean anything bad by it. Hey, some minority people use these words about themselves. How bad can they be?*

The answer is that they can be very, very bad. For many black people, the word "nigger" conjures up the whole history of slavery and discrimination that black people have endured in America. For many Jews, the word "kike" calls up visions of the pogroms and the holocaust.

Professor Richard Del Gado of Washington & Lee University emphasizes that the use of words like "nigger" and "spic" are not just expressions of contempt, or even of anger. They are tools of oppression. They are sharp reminders of the supposed low status of the people they are addressed to. They are like hammers beating the minorities down, driving them firmly into their "place" in the social structure.[1]

When minorities use these words about themselves, they do it precisely because the words hurt so much. Consciously or not, they do it to lessen the pain by claiming the terms as their own. The black comedian Dick Gregory once joked that he called a book he wrote *Nigger* to protect his mother. From then on, she wouldn't be hurt when she heard people use the word. She'd just assume they were talking about her son's book. He was joking. But his mother's hurt was real.

Many people actually do use racial and other epithets without intending any real harm. They grew up hearing Asians called "chinks," or Italians "greaseballs," and now they use the terms without even thinking about them. But the fact that no harm is intended doesn't mean that no harm is done.

If you are one of the people who use these words carelessly, learn to think before you speak. Using them in ordinary conversation shows ignorance and insensitivity, at best. Minority members who hear them are likely to be hurt and angry. Bigots who hear them will be that much more convinced that "everyone" agrees with their prejudices.

Even when these words are used (as they are in this book) only to describe other people's attitudes, they can be easily misunderstood. They are like defective hand grenades. They can explode without warning, and do unexpected harm. In most circumstances, it is better to avoid them altogether.

Ethnic Jokes

Ethnic jokes can be as dangerous as racial epithets. Since they are based on racial stereotypes, they tend to reinforce these stereotypes in the minds of people who hear them.

Nonetheless, almost everyone has heard—and laughed at—ethnic jokes. Most of us have even told them. Not because they're insulting, but because we think they're *funny*. Many people delight in telling such jokes about their own ethnic group. After all, most of them seem harmless enough.

And yet, jokes like these can be very hurtful. Those who hear them are likely to take them as an attack on the group involved, however mild that attack might be. If the listeners belong to the group joked about, they might be offended. If they do not, they might assume that the joke teller is bigoted.

How can we tell if something we say is offensive? Ann Zangig, who works with the antidiscrimination program at the University of Wisconsin, suggests that if a joke or a comment "hurts" someone, or is "demeaning" to them, then it's over the line.[2] The trouble is that it's often impossible to know whether someone will feel hurt or demeaned until the damage has already been done. This kind of standard suggests that it is best to say nothing that might be misunderstood.

Other people feel that sensitivity to racial and ethnic humor has already gone too far. The comedian and talk-show host Dennis Miller complains that college campuses are "like a minefield for comedians"[3] these days. It's all but impossible to tell a joke to a college audience without offending some group or other.

Comedians like Miller argue that we might be taking such jokes far too seriously—or maybe not seriously enough. They say that a certain amount of racial and ethnic humor might even be healthful. Laughing about our troubles is one way of making them seem lighter. Besides, they insist, instead of reinforcing stereotypes, many ethnic jokes demonstrate how silly the stereotypes really are.

But this is sensitive emotional territory, and the risk of seriously offending someone is very great. The risk of spreading stereotypes might be even greater.

Be Intolerant of Intolerance

It's not enough just to keep from spreading prejudice. It is also necessary to oppose it. Combating prejudice is like swimming against a tide. If you're not making progress, you're moving backward.

Talk to your friends and family about these issues. Make your concerns and attitudes clear. Your parents are a good place to start. Without being self-righteous about it, you can make clear to people that you do not like bigoted remarks, and will not let them go without challenging them.

Every time someone makes bigoted remarks in your presence, and you stay silent, you help to reinforce their bigotry. They will assume that you share the prejudice they are expressing, and so will everyone else within hearing. This puts you on the side of the bigots. What's more, it helps to convince everyone there that prejudice and bigotry are the norm.

Suppose you're at a party, and a girl you know makes a grossly racist remark. You are offended, but too shy to say anything about it. You don't want to be branded a weirdo or, worse, a goody-goody. You hope that someone else shoots down the speaker, but nobody does, and the conversation moves on.

You might feel a little guilty about not speaking up, but you're relieved as well. After all, nobody else objected to the comment, and if you'd said anything, you would have been isolated. Obviously, everyone else in the group shared the bigot's racist attitude, right?

Well, maybe so. But maybe not. Other people might have been just as offended as you were. Maybe everyone was, but they were just as reluctant as you were to speak out. Your silence only reinforces their mistaken idea that everybody else agrees with the bigot, just as their silence reinforces yours. Your mutual silence produces a social atmosphere in which bigotry can flourish.

On the other hand, if you speak up, others might speak up as well. This will help to create a very different kind of atmosphere, one in which tolerance, rather than bigotry, will find it easy to grow.

Does this kind of outspokenness do any good? Can it really accomplish anything? Yes, it can, according to Dr. Fletcher Blanchard of Smith College. Only "[a] few outspoken people who are vigorously anti-racist can establish the kind of social climate that discourages racist acts."[4]

One way or another, you are bound to have an influence on the attitudes of people around you. "People conform," says Dr. Stuart Cook, of the University of Colorado. If people around them use ethnic slurs, and racist epithets, they are likely to do the same. And if people around them don't express racist attitudes, they are less likely to themselves.

What's more, according to Dr. Cook, once people stop expressing bigoted attitudes, they might actually become less bigoted. This is because what we say, and how we behave, affects the way we think and feel. In the long run, says Dr. Cook, people tend to "change their beliefs to fit their behavior in order to relieve that tension that comes from feeling one way and acting another."[5]

In other words, if people talk like racists, they tend to become racists. But the reverse is just as true. People conform to tolerance as much as they conform to bigotry. Since what you do will make a difference, make sure that the difference you make is in the right direction.

Encouraging Tolerance in Your School

The measures discussed so far have been personal. They involve things that you can do in your own circle of family, friends, and acquaintances. But you can also get involved in the broader battle against prejudice, both in your school and in the community at large.

At school, reach out to students in other ethnic groups. Be open and friendly with them. When they are right, be willing to take their side in classroom disputes. Try to be a bridge between them and members of your own group. Your efforts may not be appreciated by either side at first. But, in time, you might find that you can be a real factor in improving racial and ethnic relations in your school.

There is only so much you can do alone, however. If you are serious about making an effort to overcome prejudice, seek out opportunities to work with others.

Some high schools and colleges already have programs that help to counteract prejudice. These include skits, talks, and other presentations that introduce students to other groups and cultures, and "sensitize" them to ethnic tensions. Also, there are peer-mediation programs, in which students who have conflicts with each other sit down with a neutral student and negotiate their disputes, and human relations clubs, in which students of different backgrounds are encouraged to meet and rap with each other.

Human Relations Clubs

Human relations clubs can be an effective tool for breaking down the walls that groups build between each other. They provide opportunities, in the words of Joe Giordano, to "get people comfortable talking about issues of ethnicity and race."[6] They give them a setting in which it's OK to talk about sensitive subjects like stereotypes, bigotry, and racial tensions.

Outside this kind of safe setting, most of us feel too frightened, or too insecure, to talk about such things. "When I'm talking to somebody of color," a white University of Wisconsin student told a CBS television program, "I feel I have to really word it right or they're going to be, like, 'What do you mean by that? Are you prejudiced?' And it really clams me up. I wish I could just talk to people the way I want to."[7] Human relations clubs help you do just that.

Getting a Program Started

If you're interested in making a real difference in your school, find out if it already has a human relations club, or any of the other programs mentioned above. If it does, get involved. If it doesn't, you might try to start one. Approach your school principal, or a faculty member you think might be sympathetic. Explain your concerns about intolerance and what you think might be done in your school. Suggest bringing in outside speakers, introducing peer mediation, or starting a human relations club.

Don't expect things to go smoothly. Such programs cannot be established overnight. There are bound to be problems. School officials are likely to resist doing anything that might "stir up trouble." Peer mediation requires finding someone to train student mediators. And students may not see the point of joining a human relations club.

"Sometimes it's not easy," says Eric Johnson, director of a Community Relations program in Montgomery County, Maryland. "It takes a lot of work on the part of the students and the teacher sponsor to recruit other students . . . [and] talk them into it."[8] And there is no guarantee of success. One student Johnson knows of worked for a year and a half to get a human relations club started in his school, only to fail in the end. But others have succeeded.

Johnson advises students to be both positive and persistent. Be upbeat when talking to school officials about your idea. Talk about what it can accomplish for your fellow students and the school community. If you approach school officials with an angry, demanding attitude, they won't see your idea as a way to relieve tensions, but as something that might make them worse.

Be upbeat in talking to your fellow students, too, particularly those from different racial and ethnic backgrounds. Identify people from varied backgrounds who might make good mediators or members of a human relations club, and get to work recruiting them. If a human relations club is going to be useful, it needs a diverse membership. And yet, Johnson says, minority students might be reluctant to join at first. They might not see what's in it for them. He suggests sitting down with them, one to one, in the cafeteria or elsewhere. Let them know how important they will be to the club. Let them know how much they are needed.

With this kind of hard work, and a lot of persistence, you might succeed in forging an important weapon in the battle against prejudice in your school.

Working in the Larger Community

Different communities have different problems and different needs. They also provide different opportunities for joining in the battle against prejudice. There are several places you can go to find out what's already being done in your home town.

Many communities have Human Relations Commissions, which try to defuse ethnic tensions and promote interracial goodwill. These commissions are often agencies of the county government, but some are under the local or state governments instead. Check your phone book or call city hall to find out whether your locality has one. If it does, the commission is one of the first places to go for ideas about what you can do to get active in fighting prejudice.

The typical Human Relations Commission is made up of community leaders in business, labor, religion, and education. It sponsors speaking engagements by minority representatives, workshops, and other programs that promote intercultural understanding. It intervenes in local situations where racial or other tensions are high, and offers training and support for other organizations that deal with discrimination, hate crimes, and ethnic tensions.

Some Human Relations Commissions are extremely vigorous. Others are relatively inactive. Montgomery County, Maryland, has one of the most active

Human Relations Commissions in the country. Among other programs, it runs a Network of Teens, whose teenage members reach out to offer help and emotional support to other teens victimized by harassment or hate violence. A separate Network of Neighbors program does the same for adults.

If your community suffers from hate violence, check with your Human Relations Commission or local government to see if there's a similar network in your area. If there isn't, suggest that one be started. Any community interested in establishing such an organization can contact the Montgomery County Human Relations Commission for advice.

Human Relations Camps

Another innovative project of the Montgomery Commission is a Human Relations Camp, where teenagers from different races and ethnic groups meet for a "weekend experience in interracial and intercultural understanding."[9] A sample session included teenagers of Italian, Polish, Vietnamese, Cambodian, African, Russian, Caribbean, El Salvadoran, and African-American ancestry.

Similar camps have been set up in other places, including one near Carson City, Nevada, called Anytown USA. These camps are valuable for any young person who wants a better understanding of people of different backgrounds. But they are particularly valuable for teens who have never before met people of other races as individual human beings. Student evaluations of the camps reveal some of the shock, and excitement, of learning that "they" can also be "us."

"I learned that I could make friends with people I usually wouldn't even talk to," one camper wrote.

"This camp helped me trust people," wrote another. "I learned how important it is to be honest," wrote a third. "To trust yourself as well as others."[10]

These camps inspire some teens to become more active in their own communities. Seventeen-year-old Savra Frounfelker returned from her Anytown USA experience to join with students from other local schools to found Teens Against Racial Prejudice in her hometown of Reno, Nevada. The organization's purpose, she told the Reno *Gazette-Journal*, was "to make the community aware that racism does exist in Reno. It seems like people just don't want to admit that it's here."[11] The same could be said about too many people in too many other communities around the country.

The mayor of Reno was so impressed with the teens' efforts that he honored TARP's kickoff at the local Human Rights Day celebrations.

Other Sources of Information

If your community has an inactive Human Relations Commission, or none at all, there are other places you can go. Local churches are often in the vanguard of the fight for human rights, particularly in southern communities. A church in your own neighborhood might be involved right now. Check your local churches to see if they have any projects you might be able to help with.

The local or state branch of the NAACP, or National Association for the Advancement of Colored People, is another good place to find out what's being done in your area, as well as what you can do to help.

Many communities have local citizens' groups that combat prejudice in a variety of ways. They include the Fairfield United Action (in Jenkinsville, S.C.), the Coalition Against Racist Violence (Contra Costa,

CA), and the Council of Good Will (in various other communities).[12]

You should be careful, however, about joining groups you know nothing about. Some groups have very misleading names. A northern-Wisconsin organization that calls itself Protect Americans' Rights and Resources, for example, is really devoted to eliminating the treaty rights of Native Americans.

Writing Letters to Newspapers

One effective way to affect the social climate in your community is to write letters to your local newspaper. Most papers print letters from their readers on issues of social concern, and you can take advantage of this opportunity to spread the message of tolerance.

Here are a few tips to keep in mind. They will make your letter more effective, and raise the odds that it will be published.

1. Keep your letter short. Many papers have length limitations. If your letter is too long, the editors either won't print it at all or they'll cut it down to size. In the process, they might distort what you're trying to say.

2. Limit your letter to one key point or issue. A letter to the editor is more like a poster than an essay.

3. If possible, relate your letter to a recent news story or editorial that appeared in the paper, or even to a previously published letter. Editors like letters to be relevant.

4. Write your letter carefully, and rewrite it at least once. The better it is written, the more likely it is to be published, and the more persuasive it will be to readers.

Becoming Politically Active

There is no space here to discuss the wide variety of political issues that relate to prejudice. Affirmative action, desegregation, and hate-speech laws are just a few of them. If you are seriously interested in improving the racial and ethnic climate in America, however, you should learn as much as you can about these issues.

Once you decide what you think about them, look for opportunities to become politically active. Support political causes that promote tolerance, understanding, and the rights of minorities. Work for candidates who stand for the things you believe in. Don't worry that you're too young, or that the candidate will not be interested in your help. There is always something you can do, and political candidates are always in need of volunteers.

Writing Letters to Legislators

One of the most effective things that you can do politically is also one of the easiest. Write a letter to government officials and legislators, lobbying them to support bills and policies that help to curb prejudice. Let them know what's important to you. When a bill comes up that will have an impact on the rights of minorities, tell them which way you want them to vote. After all, they work for you. You can be sure that the bigots will be making their views known. You need to be a voice on the other side.

Here are some tips on writing to legislators:

1. If you live in the legislator's district, say so. If you've voted for him or her, or worked as a volunteer in their campaign, mention that too. But don't worry if you're not yet old enough to vote. You will be soon—and, to a politician, future elections matter more than past ones do.

2.   Explain why the issue is important to you. If you're writing about a school-desegregation matter, for example, explain that as a student you want to be sure that all students have a chance for the best possible education.

3.   Always ask the official to do something specific, and make sure what you're asking is within the official's power. Don't waste a state legislator's time asking her to vote for a bill that's coming up in the U.S. Congress. Don't waste a Congressperson's time asking him to sponsor a bill that's already been passed.

4.   Be sure to ask the official to explain his or her own position on the issue. Knowing it will help you decide whether or not to vote for that person in the future. What's more, if the official has not yet taken a firm stand, your question might force him or her to come to terms with it for the first time.

Letters to any United States Senator can be addressed:

> Senator (Name)
> c/o United States Senate
> Washington, D.C. 20510

Letters to any United States Congressperson can be addressed:

> The Honorable (Name)
> c/o The United States House
> of Representatives
> Washington, D.C. 20510

For the names and addresses of your state and local officials, call the offices of the level of government involved.

Prejudice is never going to disappear entirely, any more than anger, fear, and greed are ever going to disappear. Like them, prejudice is a basic human weakness. But each of us can overcome our personal prejudices—just as we can overcome anger, fear, and greed—if we are willing to work at it.

If enough of us work at it hard enough, we can overcome the prejudices in our society as well. We might not be able to eliminate all traces of bigotry and discrimination, but we can reduce their effects, and lower the level of tension that divides us.

We can make things better, or we can make things worse. It's up to us.

A FINAL LESSON FROM HISTORY: MARCH 16, 1968

Twenty-three years to the day before Latasha Harlins was shot down in the Empire Liquor Market on South Figueroa Street, an even more tragic incident occurred half a world away. It was on that day—March 16, 1968—that the soldiers of Charlie Company, of the Americal Division of the U.S. Army, marched into a small Vietnamese village that was identified on Army maps as My Lai 4.

According to an official U.S. Army report, the members of Charlie Company were completely typical of young American soldiers. They came from the Midwest, the Northeast, the South, and the West. Most were between eighteen and twenty-one years old. Many had been sitting in high school only the year before. Just under half of them were white, and about the same number black. A few were Hispanic. At least one was Asian-American. There were Protestants among them, and also Catholics, Jews, and Mormons.

What's more, the Army report would conclude, "they brought with them [into My Lai 4] the diverse traits, prejudices and attitudes typical of the various regions of the country and segments of society from which they came."[1]

Some of "the prejudices and attitudes" they carried with them were racial: the soldiers commonly referred to the people of Viet Nam as "gooks," and "slopes," and "dinks." Some were political: they were convinced that the village was full of Communists. And some were just the inevitable prejudices of war. To the men of Charlie Company, the villagers were not really men, women, and children at all. They were *the enemy*.

Charlie Company entered the little village expecting to find and kill members of the enemy Viet Cong. Instead, they found mostly women, children, and old men. Reacting with rage and frustration, they began to massacre the innocent villagers. Within a few hours, they had slaughtered more than five hundred. The specific number is disputed. The fact of the slaughter is not.

Among the dead were several infants. Some had been shot, some bayoneted, and some beaten to death. Several of the victims might have been sympathizers of the Viet Cong, but certainly not the babies. And none of the villagers they killed, young or old, represented any immediate danger to the American soldiers that day.

How could these typical young Americans do such a horrible thing? No good answer has ever been found. Perhaps there can be no good answer. Certainly, there can never be a moral justification for such terrible acts. But one thing is clear. Without the prejudices "they brought with them," the massacre could never have taken place.

One of the most brutal of the killers, Lt. William Calley, told Army psychiatrists that "He did not feel as if he were killing human beings, but rather that they were animals with whom he could not speak or reason."[2] This is as good a definition of bigotry as any: to see people who are different, not as human beings, but as animals. *They are not like me. I am not like them.*

The men of Charlie Company were not the only Americans to feel that way. As another American soldier, who was not at My Lai, explained to a journalist, "The trouble is, no one sees the Vietnamese as people.... Therefore, it doesn't matter what you do to them."[3]

Most of us will never carry our prejudices to such murderous extremes. But it is important for each of us to realize that a group of typical young Americans did just that, one day in March 1968. It is important because the little manifestations of prejudice we see around us can often seem harmless and insignificant. It is so easy to ignore them, and to tell ourselves that prejudice is not such a big deal, really. But this is an illusion.

Followed to the end, prejudice is a road that leads straight to My Lai 4.

ORGANIZATIONS
TO CONTACT

The following organizations are all active in one way or another in the battle against prejudice.

American Arab Anti-
   Discrimination Committee
4201 Connecticut Ave. NW
Suite 500
Washington, D.C. 20008

B'nai B'rith
1640 Rhode Island Ave. NW
Washington, D.C. 20036

Center for Democratic Renewal
PO Box 50469
Atlanta, GA 30302

Japanese American
   Citizens League
1001 Connecticut Ave. NW
Suite 704
Washington, D.C. 20036

Montgomery County (MD)
   Human Relations Commission
164 Rollins Avenue
Rockville, MD 20852-4067

National Association
   for the Advancement of
   Colored People
4805 Mt. Hope Drive
Baltimore, MD 21215

National Catholic
   Conference for
   Interracial Justice
3033 Fourth St. NE
Washington, D.C. 20017

People United to Serve
   Humanity (Operation PUSH)
930 E. 50th Street
Chicago, IL 60615

The Southern Poverty
   Law Center
400 Washington Ave.
Montgomery, AL 36104

SOURCE NOTES

Chapter One: A Killing on South Figueroa Street

1. This account of the killing of Latasha Harlins is based on contemporary news reports of the trial, particularly the following articles in the *Los Angeles Times*: "Videotape Shows Teen Being Shot After Fight," by Andrea Ford, Oct. 1, 1991; "911, TV Tapes Tell Different Tales in Killing of Teen-Ager," by Andrea Ford, Oct. 2, 1991; "Grocer is Convicted in Teen Killing," by Andrea Ford and Tracy Wilkinson, Oct. 12, 1991; "Many Find Verdict Fair, But There Is Still Outrage," by Jesse Katz and Frank Clifford, *Los Angeles Times*, Oct. 12, 1991; "Korean Grocer Who Killed Black Teen Gets Probation," by Tracy Wilkinson and Frank Clifford, Nov. 16, 1991; and "Prospects for Successful Appeal of Grocer's Sentence Seen as Slim," by Dean E. Murphy, Nov. 26, 1991.

2. Andrea Ford and Tracy Wilkinson, "Grocer is Convicted in Teen Killing," *Los Angeles Times*, Oct. 12, 1991.

3. Dean E. Murphy, "Prospects for Successful Appeal of Grocer's Sentence Seen as Slim," *Los Angeles Times*, Nov. 26, 1991.

4. Ibid.

5. Tracy Wilkinson and Frank Clifford, "Korean Grocer Who Killed Black Teen Gets Probation," *Los Angeles Times*, Nov. 16, 1991.

6. Jesse Katz and Frank Clifford, "Many Find Verdict Fair, But There Is Still Outrage," *Los Angeles Times*, Oct. 12, 1991.

7. Haya el Nasser, "Calif. Judge's Tough Trial," USA *Today*, January 10, 1992.

8. Ibid.

9. Tracy Wilkinson and Frank Clifford, "Korean Grocer Who Killed Black Teen Gets Probation," Nov. 16, 1991.

10. Ibid.

11. Emily MacFarquhar, "Fighting Over the Dream," U.S. *News & World Report,* May 18, 1992, p. 34.

Chapter Two: An Introduction to Prejudice

1. Quoted by Krista Ramsey, Gannett News Service, "Prejudice: It Often Takes a Shock to Change Attitudes," *Wausau Daily Herald,* Sept. 9, 1991.

2. *Webster's New World Dictionary of the American Language,* Second College Edition. David B. Guralink, Ed. in Chief. (New York: Simon & Schuster, 1980), p. 1122.

3. *The Shorter Oxford English Dictionary,* Vol. II, prepared by William Little and others. (Oxford: Clarendon Press, 1969), p. 1569.

4. *Webster's,* p. 1122.

5. Gordon W. Allport. *The Nature of Prejudice.* (Reading, MA: Addison-Wesley, 1954), p. 8.

6. James F. Calhoun and Joan Ross Acocella. *Psychology of Adjustment and Human Relationships.* (New York: Random House, 1978), pp. 241–42.

7. *The National Prejudice Puzzle Call-In,* NPR, Sept. 15, 1990.

Chapter Three: Racial, Religious, and Ethnic Prejudices

1. Holmes, Fred B. *Prejudice and Discrimination,* p. 5.

2. In the Foreword to Michael Billig's *Psychology, Racism & Fascism.* A Searchlight pamphlet. (Birmingham, England: Searchlight, 1979), page unnumbered.

3. Joan Beck, "Anthropologists Discount Racial Classification," *The State,* Columbia, S.C., March 17, 1991.

4. Van den Berghe, Pierre L. *Race and Racism: A Comparative Perspective.* (New York: John Wiley and Sons, 1967), p. 11.

5. Holmes, p. 5.

6. Van den Berghe, p. 12.

7. "Nominee's Wife Has Own Foes," *Milwaukee Sentinel,* Sept. 11, 1991.

8. "You Can't Join Their Clubs," *Newsweek,* June 10, 1991, p. 48.

9. Marilyn Elias, Gannett News Service, "Inter-Race Adoptees Grow Up Healthy, Aware," *Wausau Sunday Herald*, August 18, 1991.

10. Caroline Wachira, of Coral Gables, Florida, in a letter to *Glamour* magazine, April, 1992, p. 32.

11. Elias.

12. *Racism: Points of View*. MTV Television, 1991.

13. Jack Newfield was speaking at an editorial board meeting of the *New York Post*, April 2, 1992, cablecast over the C-SPAN Television Network.

14. Cary Segall, "State Court to Review Hate Crimes Law," *Wisconsin State Journal*, Feb. 23, 1992.

15. "Cultural Clashes Boost Hate Crime Reports," *Milwaukee Journal*, Sept. 9, 1991.

16. Gordon W. Allport, *The Nature of Prejudice*. (Reading, MA: Addison-Wesley, 1954), p. 444.

17. *Blood in the Face*. A documentary film, produced and directed by Anne Bohlen, Kevin Rafferty, James Ridgeway. Right Thinking Productions, 1991.

18. For example, "Jesus Was No Jew!" by James Combs, reprinted from *Christian Vanguard*, Feb., 1972, in *The Racist Reader* (Anoka, MN: Greenhaven Press, 1974), pp. 76–83.

19. Leonard Zeskind. *The "Christian Identity" Movement: Analyzing Its Theological Rationalization for Racist and Anti-Semitic Violence*. (Atlanta: Center for Democratic Renewal, 1986), pp. 16–17.

20. Shirer, William. *The Rise and Fall of the Third Reich*. (New York: Fawcett, 1960), p. 1256.

21. Article on the "Holocaust," *Funk & Wagnalls New Encyclopedia*, Volume 13.

Chapter Four: Causes of Prejudice

1. Thomas Sowell. *Ethnic America*. (New York: Basic Books, 1981), p. 290.

2. Ricardo Chavira, Sylvester Monroe, and Richard Woodbury, "Browns vs. Blacks," *Time*, July 29, 1991, p. 15.

3. "Prejudice in Intercultural Communication," *Intercultural Communication: A Reader*, p. 355.

4. According to Joe Girodano, *National Prejudice Puzzle Call-In*, National Public Radio, Sept. 15, 1991.

5. Doug Clark. "Former Racist Returns to Say 'I'm Sorry.'" *Spokesman Review*, Sept. 21, 1986.

6. *Beyond Hate*, copyright, Public Affairs Television, and International Cultural Programming, Inc., 1991. Broadcast over PBS in May, 1991.

Chapter Five: Stereotypes
1. Walter Lippmann. *Public Opinion*. (New York: Harcourt Brace, 1922). Quoted in Allport, p. 191.

2. Waltrud G. Karkar. ... *And They Danced On*. (Wausau, WI: Aardvark, 1989), p. 18.

3. *Scholastic Update*, September 20, 1991, p. 13.

4. "Civil Rights: Voices 1991," USA *Weekend*, June 28–30, 1991, p. 17.

5. *The Chicago Tribune*, Jan. 21, 1992.

6. U.S. Bureau of Census figures, *The World Almanac and Book of Facts*, 1992. (New York: Pharos Books, 1992), p. 77.

7. Sophonia Scott Gregory, "The Hidden Hurdle," *Time*, March 16, 1992, p. 44.

8. *The World Almanac and Book of Facts*, 1990. (New York: World Almanac, 1990), p. 190.

9. Jim Meyers, "What's the Difference? Studies Inconclusive." USA *Today*, December 16, 1991.

Chapter Six: "You've Got to Be Taught"
1. Quoted in "Learning Prejudice," *Scholastic Update*, April 7, 1989, p. 8.

2. *Intercultural Theory and Practice: Perspectives on Education, Training, and Research*. Richard W. Brislin. Quoted in Larry A. Samovar and Richard E. Porter's *Prejudice in Intercultural Communication: A Reader*. (Belmont, CA: Wadsworth, 1982), p. 355.

3. James F. Calhoun and Joan Ross Acocella. *Psychology of Adjustment and Human Relationships*, p. 279.

4. This is how Hanover United for Equality, Diversity and Nonviolence explained its choice of "Exploring Generations of Preju-

dice" as the theme for a conference in 1991. *The Monitor*, Dec. 1991, p. 22.

5. D. Bem. *Beliefs, Attitudes, and Human Affairs*. (Monterey, CA: Brooks/Cole, 1970), p. 75.

6. Calhoun and Acocella, pp. 279–80.

7. Goleman, Daniel. "New Way to Battle Bias: Fight Acts, Not Feelings," *New York Times*, July 17, 1991.

8. See *Hate Violence and White Supremacy: A Decade Review. 1980–1990*. A Klanwatch Intelligence Report, published by the Southern Poverty Law Center, December, 1989.

9. *All Things Considered*. National Public Radio, Feb. 10, 1992.

10. Jon Wiener. "Racial Hatred on Campus," *The Nation*, February 27, 1989, p. 260.

11. Quoted by Jeff Coplon, in "Skinhead Nation," *Rolling Stone*, December 1, 1988.

12. Goleman.

13. Democratic Presidential Candidate Forum, College Park, Maryland, Mar. 1, 1992, cablecast on the C-SPAN Cable Television Network.

14. Ibid.

15. USA *Weekend*, p. 7.

16. CNN Television News report, January 31, 1991.

17. CNN Television News report, January 24, 1991.

18. USA *Weekend*, p. 17.

19. Pedro de Mesones, quoted in USA *Weekend*, p. 17.

Chapter Seven: What's So Bad About Prejudice, Anyway?

1. Based on figures from *Health United States 1990*, a report of the U.S. Department of Health and Human Services, reported in "Health Gap: Blacks Lag in Life Expectancy," in USA *Today*, April 8, 1991.

2. "The Unsteady State of Black America," *St. Petersburg Times*, January 27, 1992.

3. Gerson Antell, Walter Harris, William S. Dobkin. *Current Issues in American Democracy.* (New York: Amsco, 1992), p. 226.

4. All the figures up to this point in the paragraph come from *Health United States.*

5. National Public Radio news report, March 24, 1992.

6. *Health United States.*

7. Edith Folb, "Who's Got Room at the Top?", *Intercultural Communication: A Reader,* p. 137.

8. Marcus Mabry, with Patrick Rogers, "Bias Begins at Home," *Time,* August 5, 1991, p. 33.

9. "Producing a Paler Shade of Skin Color," USA *Today,* December 2, 1991.

10. Quoted by Tina Burnside, "Self-hate, Hopelessness Lead to Violence," *Milwaukee Sentinel,* November 27, 1990.

11. Tom Squitieri, "Slayings Set Record in '91; No End in Sight," USA *Today,* January 7, 1992.

12. Quoted by Burnside.

13. James F. Calhoun, and Joan Ross Acocella. *Psychology of Adjustment and Human Relationships.* (New York: Random House, 1978), p. 242.

14. *Beyond Hate.*

15. Daniel Levitas of the Center for Democratic Renewal, quoted in "America's Youthful Bigots," U.S. *News & World Report,* May 7, 1990, p. 59.

16. "Hate Crime Laws: How Are They Doing?" *The Monitor,* December, 1991, p. 18.

17. Cary Segall. "State Court to Review Hate Crimes Law," *Wisconsin State Journal,* Feb. 23, 1992.

18. Sen. Paul Tsongas, speaking at a town meeting in Manchester, New Hampshire, Feb. 10, 1992, cablecast over the C-SPAN Television Network.

19. Senator Bill Bradley (Dem.-N.J.), speaking in the U.S. Senate, and quoted in "Sen. Bradley's Question," *The Philadelphia Enquirer,* July 12, 1991.

Chapter Eight: Working to Overcome
Our Prejudices

1. Joe Giordano, *National Prejudice Puzzle Call-In*, National Public Radio, Sept. 15, 1990.

2. Elizabeth Brixey, "Fabu Mogaka," *Wisconsin State Journal*, Feb. 23, 1992.

3. Edward T. Hall and William Foote Whyte, "Intercultural Communication: A Guide to Men of Action." *Human Organization*, XVIV, 1960, p. 10.

4. "A Violent Death in a Violent Nation," *The Atlanta Journal*, March 27, 1991.

Chapter Nine: Overcoming Despair

1. " 'The Lure of Excuses,' " *Newsweek*, July 29, 1991, p. 27.

2. Elizabeth Brixey, "Fabu Mogaka," *Wisconsin State Journal*, Feb. 23, 1992.

3. See Drew T. Brown, *You Gotta Believe*. (New York: Avon, 1992).

4. National Press Club Symposium on Race Relations and Politics, Sept. 5, 1991, cablecast by the C-SPAN Television Network. The speaker was Peter Brown, Chief editorial writer of Scripps-Howard newspapers.

5. Sophronia Scott Gregory, "The Hidden Hurdle," *Time*, March 16, 1992, p. 45.

Chapter Ten: Working to Overcome
the Prejudices of Others

1. Interviewed on *Clark and Company*, Wisconsin Public Radio Network, Oct. 7, 1991.

2. Interviewed by author, Jan. 24, 1992.

3. *Dennis Miller Show*, Fox Television, January 31, 1992.

4. Goleman, Daniel. "New Way to Battle Bias: Fight Acts, Not Feelings," *New York Times*, July 17, 1991.

5. Ibid.

6. *National Prejudice Puzzle Call-In*, National Public Radio Network, Sept. 15, 1991.

7. *Faces of Hate*, CBS Television News, 1991.

8. Interviewed by author, Jan. 31, 1992.

9. Eric P. Johnson, "Camping for Cultural Understanding," *National Institute Against Prejudice and Violence Forum*, Dec. 1988, p. 2.

10. The quotes from camp evaluations were provided by the Montgomery County Human Relations commission.

11. Ron Fitten, "High School Student Group Fights Racism," Reno *Gazette-Journal*, date unknown.

12. These, and other, antiprejudice groups are mentioned in *When Hate Comes to Town: A Handbook of Model Community Responses.* (Atlanta, GA; The Center for Democratic Renewal, 1986).

A Final Lesson from History
March 16, 1968

1. Quoted by Michael Bilton and Kevin Sim. *Four Hours in My Lai,* (New York: Viking, 1992), p. 51.

2. Psychiatrist's report, quoted in Bilton and Sim, p. 336.

3. The reporter was Jonathan Schell. The soldier's comment is quoted in Bilton and sim, p. 60.

FOR FURTHER READING

Books

Allport, Gordon W. *The Nature of Prejudice*. (Reading, MA: Addison-Wesley, 1954)

Dunbar, Leslie W. *Minority Report—What Has Happened to Blacks, Hispanics, American Indians and Other Minorities in the Eighties*. (New York: Pantheon Books, 1984)

Gay, Kathlyn. *The Rainbow Effect: Interracial Families*. (New York: Franklin Watts, 1987)

Kronenwetter, Michael. *United They Hate*. (New York: Walker, 1992)

McKissack, Patricia and Fredrick. *Taking a Stand Against Racism and Racial Discrimination*. (New York: Franklin Watts, 1990)

McNickle, D'Arcy. *They Came Here First. The Epic of the American Indian*. Rev. Ed. (New York: Octagon, 1975)

Sowell, Thomas. *Ethnic America*. (New York: Basic Books, 1981)

Tateishi, John. *And Justice for All: An Oral History of the Japanese American Detention Camps*. (New York: Random House, 1984)

Terkel, Studs. *Race: How Blacks and Whites Think and Feel About the American Obsession*. (New York: New Press, 1992)

Articles

Burnside, Tina. "Self-hate, Hopelessness Lead to Violence," *Milwaukee Sentinel*, November 27, 1990.

Goleman, Daniel. "New Way to Battle Bias: Fight Acts, Not Feelings," *New York Times*, July 17, 1991.

Gregory, Sophonia Scott. "The Hidden Hurdle," *Time*, March 16, 1992, p. 44.

Mabry, Marcus, with Patrick Rogers. "Bias Begins at Home," *Time*, August 5, 1991.

Minerbrook, Scott, with Miriam Horn. "Side by Side, Apart: The Difficult Search for Racial Peace in Brooklyn," U.S. *News & World Report*, Nov. 4, 1991.

INDEX